KEEP IT TI

History of the Making of The East Coast Truckers Children's Convoy.

By Glenn D. Johnson.

With contributions from others.

COMPILED & EDITED

By

SHEILA HUTCHINSON

Front Cover Photograph:
Glenn Johnson's lead truck on the first truckers Children's Convoy from Repton House in 1986.

Back Cover Photograph:
The 26th Children's Convoy with Rob Billman, the chairman of the ECTC, in front position on the A47 near Acle. (Hutchinson)

ISBN 9780954168391

Published
By
Sheila & Paul Hutchinson,
7 Colman Avenue,
Stoke Holy Cross,
Norwich,
Norfolk.
NR14 8NA

Email: paul.sheila844@btinternet.com

Printed
By
Really Useful Print Co. Ltd.
Bessemer Road,
Norwich.

Acknowledgements

I wish to thank all of the East Coast Truckers Committee Members and the Charity Trustees for their help in producing this book.

A part of Glenn Johnson's story was serialized previously in the East Coast Truckers Charity News. The articles by David Land and Teresa Wilce were also previously published in the magazine and I thank the editors of the magazine, Mike Read and Ivan Hardy, and the Charity for permission to use these writings.

Particular thanks go to Glenn Johnson, Rob Billman, David Land, Teresa Wilce, Peter Wright, Mike Read, Susan Alabaster, Nick Ireland and Betty Tortice for their contributions.

The East Coast Truckers' Committee in 2011:

The East Coast Truckers' websites:

www.eastcoastrtickers.org
www.keeptheconvoyalive.info

EDITOR'S INTRODUCTION.

In June 2011, I was asked along to the East Coast Truckers' Charity Fete at Halvergate by Betty Tortice. While I was there, I was asked to put together a book about the Truckers. Since then I have met up with some of the truckers who have kindly contributed to this book.

The truckers and all of the many volunteers work hard together giving up their free time to arrange convoys, Christmas parties and various other outings for disadvantaged children who look forward to their special treats.

This is their story.

Sheila Hutchinson

CONTENTS   Page

PREFACE BY THE ECTC CHAIRMAN ROB BILLMAN

HOW DID THIS START?

Imagine this, one sunny August Sunday morning, in 1986. Everything in the city of Norwich was calm and tranquil, the birds are singing and then some fella decides to start blowing his air horns on his truck, him and his 25 mates!!!!!! What was he thinking of!!! To this day some 25 plus years later, I still ask him the same question. The gentleman in question is Glenn Johnson. Glenn and his wife Mary had decided that instead of having a quiet bank holiday Sunday at home they and a group of truckers elected to go to the local children's home, scoop up some children and take them out for the day.

So that was the day of the first EAST COAST TRUCKERS CHILDREN'S CONVOY. Some 25 years later and it is still running: it has not been an easy road for Glenn and if the truth be known at times it was a curse. Being the founder and lead truck for 24 of the 25 always left Glenn somewhat a target, not always because of the convoy, but indirectly. When you are the driving force behind such an event, you have to be very focused and driven regardless of what may stand in your way, so at times this would get our hero into the odd scrape or two!!!!! Either way, our man was not for giving up.

Of course, the tale doesn't stop there. In the 25 years of the Children's convoy, there have been many ups and downs, new members, and new projects. Off the back of the success of the children's convoy came the East Coast Truckers Charity. This was the dawning of a new era. A status that has earned this group of well meaning truck drivers and families the respect of the public. Since the forming of the charity, they have put together more outings for disadvantaged children, provided more specialist equipment and delivered more priceless smiles than anyone could ever perceive.

5

2011 saw the purchase of 2 holiday homes on the Norfolk coast. These homes have provided an affordable week away for some 40 families in the first season.

This book is a snapshot of 25 years of blood, sweat, tears and laughter. It is based on the accounts and memories of one man, and is enhanced by the experiences shared by others. A story of some that have passed before us, those that helped shape this wonderful charity into what you see today. As the chairman and convoy director, I am very proud of where the convoy came from, how the charity was formed, but never too proud to shed a tear. I've only been here some 5 years, but like those before me, I think I've made my mark.

Rob Billman, October 2011.

KEEP IT TIGHT
By
GLENN D. JOHNSON

Dedication.

It goes without saying that this work must be dedicated to my family. While I have always had the choice about how I have spent my free time, my family was not always been afforded the same privilege, but they have all been there to offer help and support throughout the long twenty odd years to date. Mary, Neal, Dale, Damian, and much later Tracey, deserve as much thanks and credit as anybody else mentioned in this story.

Foreword.

In this book, I hope to be able to give an honest account of how I saw events and occasions unfold. While it is my view and opinion, I will, however, try to be objective and even critical of my involvement with every facet and moulding of what, after all, is a chronicle of a very famous and prestigious club.

As this story unfolds, it will be obvious to the reader that there is a long time span between start and end. I have omitted names when in my consideration offence or embarrassment could be caused to either the charity or individuals. The East Coast Truckers Club, in either of its two forms, is not responsible for the contents of this account.

4.00 am and for the umpteenth time I have pawed my way through every weather forecast that I can find. My eyes are still stinging from the lack of sleep and proper rest. Will the coming dawn bring me blue sunny skies, or will God heap just one more burden on me and my precious cargo? Just one more forecast then I will move on to the next more pressing problem, after all nothing can be changed now, we are less than a few hours away from what is the best part of a years planning. I close my eyes and quietly ask God for a successful day. I tell him my cargo has had tough luck, and if he is about and lending an ear, could he for heavens sake just give us a break. Opening my eyes I drift back to those simple days 20 years ago, how have I found myself in this so delightfully painful situation? I ask myself, why this simple deed has had such an impact on, not only my life, but also so very many other people. I will go on asking that same question until the day I die. However, we are still here, bigger and better in spite of obstacles and problems. What is the secret? Magic, Bloody Magic!

8

Let me take you back to where it all started and hope you experience some of our magic too.

Way back in the early part of the seventies, a young family was just starting out on the hazardous road of marriage and children. They lived in a dilapidated caravan, on a residential caravan site, miles from any form of civilization, at a place called Burgh Castle.

Their humble existence afforded very few luxuries and the wages of a milkman just never seemed to go far enough.

So the breadwinner of the family decided to gamble the very meagre savings that they had, on an HGV driving course, with the aim of securing a licence at the end of the course. One failed attempt and scrounging the repeat test fees from his mother saw the breadwinner finally getting an HGV license.

That was the turning point for this family; the now proud owner of a nice new HGV license applied for a job with Boulton and Paul of Norwich. The application was successful. Doubling his take home pay overnight, our young driver was not long before he could get his young wife and two-year-old child away from the damp, cold, and toilet-less mildewed caravan. He brought them to the luxury of a proper home in Norwich; they then had a relatively good life within the realms of road transport for the next few years.

Our breadwinner was, however, not quite content with his lot driving a truck for somebody else. He had a dream of running his own truck. He realized his dream in 1980; and although sometimes it had seemed a very bad move, nothing in this life will ever go entirely to plan, even with all the problems that being his own man would bring, he still looks back with very little regret.

Life for the last thirty years has not been at all bad for our once young aspiring family man, with a wish to give his flock the very best of everything he could possibly afford.

There is a larger picture to all of this. It is not my life that this story is about to depict; my life and the life of that young family are merely pawns to the cause. I was that young family man and breadwinner, with dreams and aspirations that were not always achieved; nevertheless I have to admit that The East Coast Truckers gave a sense of purpose to all that I have done.

IN THE BEGINNING.

The fairy lights on my GEC AM rig crackled into life on a dark and dismal morning way back in 1981 "Have you heard about this new club that is to be formed Sunday morning at Ebenezer's", was part of the modulation I caught the back end of. "Big ten four", came the reply from several nearby breakers, "We will eye ball you Sunday morning. Ten. Ten. Bye Bye"

I was curious and had to find out more for myself. Sunday morning found me making my way to Ebenezer's nightclub. On arrival, I found many faces well known to me. Faces I usually viewed as they thundered along on the opposite carriageway in an assortment of Volvo F88, F86, Scania LB110, LB80, ERFs, Transcontinental and Yorkie Bars, (DAF so nicked named because of a chocolate ad that featured a DAF 2800).

It had been a well-advertised and organized meeting; a trait that lived on in the club for many years to come. About 25 people had attended. A committee was formed and word would go out to every local trucker that a mass meeting would be organized for the 1st Sunday morning of the following month. The meeting was to be at the Norfolk Dumpling, Hall Road, Norwich, and so it was.

On a Sunday morning in June of 1981 over 60 truckers heralded the birth of the ECT.

The very first committee was to be Chairman Colin Carter, Treasurer Terry Thiel, and Secretary Ronnie King.

The original concept and constitution of the club was to be a kind of insurance for its members.

This was brought about by the persecution and harassment of truckers for using CB (citizen band) radios. The CBs were imported from the US and sold legally to truckers but were deemed illegal to use. (A typical gobbledygook UK law.) Bearing in mind that every rig cost around £70.00 + Twig (Today's equivalent price £180.00). This put a sizable hole in what was even then a poor wage. The persecution and harassment came in the form of an organization that came to be known as Busby. GPO, the General Post Office as it was then, was responsible for any form of wireless communication. British Telecom had recently been formed and part of their advertising campaign was a stupid cartoon bird called Busby. Busby was used as a gimmick to win people over to what was after all a monopoly (no Cellnet or Sky then!). So it came to be that the post master general waged war on any trucker using an illegal device for transmitting or receiving wireless signals.

Truckers have always been inventive and humorous and thus the phrase "I have been busted by Busby" became known.

As Busby stepped up his campaign to rid the world of criminal truck drivers talking to one another quite harmlessly it became apparent that we the truckers should stick together. (Do not get excited it did not last long.) They set up an insurance scheme where, if busted, you as a member could approach the committee and receive money to buy a replacement rig.

If you were apprehended in any one, of Busby's mini swoops or Road Blocks, your rig was confiscated and destroyed and you could receive a £500 fine. Usually your first offence you would just lose your rig.

I fondly remember one hilarious incident relating to a long gone member and a fellow called Mr. Sharp.

It is only fair to say that the term long gone is not strictly true, this particular man will crop up many times in this tale, and as I said earlier, some names are safer to leave out, the subject is still alive and kicking. I believe in all accounts he has done well for his self. I do not for one minute begrudge him that nor anything else; I just wish he could have been more of a man and less of a money machine. For in spite of all the trouble and pain he caused for me, which I now know was a direct result of his actions; I truly liked him and was never bored with his company. He was amusing, comical and quite loveable in his own inimitable way. What a pity his one big failing was his desire to control people through his ability to make money. I regret to this day losing trust and interest in this man because he would, I am sure to this day, be a very valuable asset to our newly fledged charity.

Now Mr. Sharp was a very dedicated employee of British Telecom, his immediate mandate was to carry out the Post Master Generals task of stopping the illegal use of the airways.

Mr. Sharp naturally targeted some of our members more vigorously than others. The member of the day involved heavily in this comical event, was vulnerable in and around Norwich because 90% of his driving was done in and around the City area.

One Easter bank holiday about ten families belonging to the East Coast Truckers, decided to take a camping or caravan weekend at Alton Towers Theme Park. We set out on the Saturday morning after meeting at the Round Well public house. Not long into the journey, in fact we had

11

only gone a couple of miles when somebody spotted Mr. Sharp following us.

Because we were all using the criminal device known as the CB, we were all targets of the infamous Busby.

We all scattered in various directions so he could only bust just one of us; fortunately he had no power to stop or apprehend a motor vehicle, which would mean him waiting until his intended target or victim stopped. Poor old Mr. Sharp had targeted John Hammond. What he had not bargained for was John spotting him and having the cunning and will to hang on to his C.B. come hell or high water.

The chase continued all the way to Derby city centre, some 160 miles.

Our John's family by this time had seen every backwater road between Norwich and Derbyshire and still our member could not rid himself of Mr. Sharp. Eventually Mr. Sharp had to make a fuel stop and our man was home and free.

I recall with amusement the comment John's wife made at the laugh in that evening. Pat said with pained look, "When I finally got to a toilet Niagara Falls would have had a hard time keeping up with me". We had many a good laugh about that weekend, Oh what ever happened?

The first six months of the club saw many truckers being helped and everything seemed perfect. Social functions were organized and plans for many trips and events were discussed. The truckers seemed to be forming a social side to what was now a very large membership, well exceeding 130 people. But alas it was not to last.

Only six months into the birth of the East Coast Truckers Club, many others, and I, could see that a clash of personalities and political views would one day erupt into a very unpleasant and violent confrontation. Although the club had a strong hard working membership and a dedicated clever committee, some elements of the grass root members were hell bent on turning to anarchy if they did not win a well-debated argument.

Thankfully, the day I dreaded was a long way off, but it would come as sure as the devil made ERFs.

That aside, the newly formed club was striding ahead with a multitude of social and charitable ventures.

WE DISCOVER CHARITY.

The first ever charity fundraiser was to physically pull an HGV the entire circumference of the Norwich Ring Road. On the arranged Sunday around sixty members and their families assembled at the start point, we borrowed an outfit from Anglian Windows and we completed our task with the help of the internal combustion engine only once and that understandably was on Thunder Lane. Thunder Lane is well known by the locals for its very steep incline. A great time was had by all, we collected all the money we had aimed for, and everyone agreed it had been a success.

The money raised was used to purchase portable colour televisions for the maternity unit of the Norfolk and Norwich Hospital.

The press was duly informed and they turned up at the presentation along with all the people who had made the day a success, our very first of hundreds of press

Photographs and mentions, yes the fame of the ECT had just come out of crawler gear. We were on our way.

As mentioned earlier we were a very large club by the end of our first year, just to give a rough idea of how many members we had our first ever Dinner Dance was attended by no fewer than 250 people. We had taken over the Sprowston Hall Hotel for the whole of that weekend.

The format for years to come had been cast that evening, we had a clubman of the year, we had the Wally of the year and we ran a raffle that would boost our already bulging bank account.

The club was now well into its second year and plans were afoot for an event that was to become the making and the downfall of the ECT. I was busy helping in whatever way I could to make this event as successful as possible and ultimately earned myself a place on the committee, a real privilege in those days. I was elected to be the East Coast Truckers public relations man. This post would eventually help me to set up the now world famous East Coast Truckers Children's Convoy.

The event was to be held on the bank holiday Sunday; the reasons for this were that most of the members would have to make themselves ready for work on the Monday, or at the very least, the trucks we needed to highjack for the event would be needed back by their rightful owners.

We had secured the whole of the Hewitt School playing fields and it was our intention to run what we named as THE EAST COAST TRUCKERS FUN DAY.

FUN DAYS

There are fun days all over the country now but I believe we were one of the first organizations to use this term

This was to combine member's trucks and a general bag of fun for the whole of the day.

Just to give an idea of what was in store for the paying public, they could sample what life was like in the not too common sight in those days of a super truck. They could have photographs taken in the trucks along with their families; we had various food stalls and numerous novelty stalls.

One of the stalls we aptly named as WUMP A TRUCKER. We hit upon the idea of letting Joe Public vent his anger on us innocent truckers with the theme of get your own back on that creep who carved you up last week.

The idea was that four of our members were locked in a stock like affair, Joe Public would purchase readymade bags of flour and proceed to knock the block of one of the truckers, they, forgive the pun, went like a bomb.

One of my favourite stalls of the day was the dunking stool. We had in those days some very clever members and one such member made a dunking stool, it consisted of a chair suspended over a tank of deep water.

One of our prettier and rather well endowed female members or anybody else, who fitted the bill, was made to sit in the chair suspended above the water tank. Joe public would throw bags of water into a trigger mechanism, when the trigger was at the right level the poor cow dropped unceremoniously into the water.

Oh, I forgot to mention a flimsy tee shirt was the only garment they were allowed to wear. I remember one of the gorgeous victims climbing out of the tank to roars of applause, which was the only time since that, I can remember seeing nipples on nipples.

The administration side of the event thought that in order to get maximum advertising we would need the services of a local celebrity, not only to open the FUN DAY but also to help with prize giving and general duties.

Through a city agent, we secured the services of an up and coming young DJ who was working for the newly formed BBC Radio

Norfolk. As I recall a substantial fee was negotiated and I am sure we got value for money. Ten years later that up and coming celebrity was to have a very significant effect in the future of the Children's Convoy, yes you guessed it we had our first introduction to the very amiable WALLY WEBB.

Our first really big event had at times seemed like it was going to be much more than we as humble thick truckers could handle, in so much so that people with more expertise and resources than us shuddered at what they thought we were mad to attempt.

We as the ECT have never thought anything was too big or impossible to handle and I do not think we ever will. As I write this story, we are involved with what we hope will one day be a credible alternative to that mother of all rip-offs staged annually at Peterborough.

Of our first attempt, was it a success? Yes, did we raise loads of dosh? Yes, did we all have a good time? Yes! Yes! Yes! Would we do it again? YES.

The clubs 3rd and 4th years, although good were starting to stale a little, we were still as big and as strong as ever but our ever energetic membership needed more to get their teeth into.

We had by this time completed three very good FUN DAYS the last one being held at the now disappeared Costessey High School, the theme for this day had been an incredible attempt at constructing a safe military type assault course. As I have said, we never thought small. We somehow managed to erect the whole thing one Saturday, tried it out on ourselves, did a circuit of the City centre in 10 trucks to advertise our day, complete with a gorilla running amok through all the Saturday shoppers, then Saturday evening we all got thoroughly drunk.

Oh, yes the gorilla.

Never short of ideas, we thought it is no good just handing out a few flyers to advertise our day; we have to make an impact. So up stepped a volunteer to don a rented gorilla outfit. The idea was that the gorilla was to run in front of the trucks as we made a slow but previously allowed by the police, convoy, through the city centre(something else that was to help our convoy much later on) not the gorilla, the convoy. How were we to know that the fool would over act his part and run into the assembled crowds?

People ran whichever way they could to get out of the way of our now totally out of control prat in a fur suit. It was great. The next day saw 500 people attend our FUN DAY.

We were by this stage of the club being asked by local charities to take on more and more tasks. Since the advent of the film CONVOY, every body was becoming interested in trucks and truckers. We constantly reviewed people's requests, some we could help others we just had to reject due to human resources only going so far.

For people on the outside it was difficult to make them see that because of our long hours every one of our hours was worth three, if not more of theirs. Nevertheless, we took on an incredible amount of functions. One of these I will come back in detail to, later in the story, was the HERALD OF FREE ENTERPRISE DISASTER. But one function we did adopt big time was the LORD MAYORS PROCESSION.

As usual, we had to go over the top. We the committee decided to erect a float in the theme of the old women in a shoe. Everybody put heart and soul, forgive the pun, into the construction, it took weeks laying paper mashed over a wire netting frame.

The whole thing was constructed at one of our member's farms. Every night for about twelve weeks, I would go out to Wroxham and meet with other members. We would slap on a bit of mashie and generally have a whale of a time.

As I have said before we always had fun while we were working. Not quite so much as one fellow who decided to make a play for one of the single lasses that very often helped us at night. He was caught slapping more than paper mashie, with his pants and his guard down. I do not think he is with his wife of the time now!

The float when finished was an absolute picture, all painted up and fully manned by members and their children. We thought we were sure to win something, sadly we did not but that did not matter to us we had more fun than all the other floats put together.

As for the other floats, we were at the forefront of virtually anything that was happening locally, true to form I was asked to attend the organizers meeting of the Lord Mayors Procession. Whereupon I took on the task of supplying no fewer than 20 trucks for people who had no access to the type of vehicle they wanted.

We also took on the task of collecting all of the barriers that had been put up for the evening, a task that Alison, one of our lady truckers performed right up to quite recently.

Back to our float, it was decided that it was too good just to break up so we would use it for two other local carnivals. One such carnival was to be held at Wymondham, the plonker selected to transport the float out

16

to Wymondham thought he was on an extremely tight delivery schedule. Half way down the A11 Fred Agomba, yes that is his real name, lost the top of our shoe, the other half of the float was reported to be scattered at various intervals along the rest of the A11.The guilty party, then went on to somersault several of his own trucks at numerous locations throughout the British Isles, needless to say we won't be asking him to transport any more hard fought for projects.

Our final attempt at winning the Lord Mayors Procession (although we would still help with supplying trucks and barrier erection) was a very original float depicting a racing truck loaned by one of our members, Ady Kidd and an old ERF pinched from Turners yard when they were not looking. The two trucks were ingeniously placed on a borrowed low loader. We staffed the float with an old fashioned looking driver, complete with bib and brace, also on the trailer with his posh looking race overalls was Ady, he was surrounded by a bevy of scantily clad girls, Mickey Moore the old fashioned looking driver was surrounded by ropes and sheets. Not much of a good deal Mick kept telling us. Back to the float, have you guessed the theme yet?
RACE HORSE WORK HORSE, just brilliant, well I thought it was good. As a point of interest when we delivered the ERF back to Turners, they denied owning such a pile of tat, well they would wouldn't they. Finally, just as a matter of interest, when we got to the end of the processions route guess who would be sitting in the judges stand? Our old friend WALLY WEBB.

We as a club were forever looking for much more challenging and demanding events, the fun days were deemed a general success, the social evenings were well attended, brilliantly organized and always profitable. That really adventurous event was about to be born. I would never have gotten so excited had I known how much trouble our ultimate direction would cause.

The first Sunday of every month would see us thrashing out any problem that may have arisen during the previous month. We would also announce any up and coming engagements and we would have healthy debate on a wide range of subjects. Most of the debates and discussions were conducted in a civil and amicable way. The nagging suspicion of impending trouble that I kept getting was starting to become ever more apparent. There was a very definite change of mood.

Two points of discussion were coming up repeatedly, one point I will come back to a little later because it was by most standards quite

17

trivial. The point to cause the biggest up set was the advent of the government of the day's decision to grant a legal frequency to satisfy the need for a CITIZENS BAND radio.

As usual, our illustrious government lashed the whole affair up.

Their argument against the frequency we were using illegally was that it caused interference to televisions, pagers, police band radios and it would also upset heart pace makers.

To this day, I do not know if one of my many modulations with other breakers caused a death. The whole debacle had turned into a farce.

The point to cause consternation was this, as the club was formed to safe guard against confiscation of the illegal AM frequency rigs, we should not now accept recognition of the new FM frequency. You may think now that all these arguments were trivial and childish, but at the time, emotions were running very high whenever FM rigs were mentioned.

I must agree with one-comment regards the fact that very many people had made financial sacrifices and more to get CB legalized, but nevertheless we have to move on.

The point of recognition ran on, and on, and on. Now I could see where the trouble I had feared would come from.

FIGHT TIME.

Two very prominent members, one of who would eventually cause the break-up of the club, had a very verbal and heated exchange regards the FM rig. The instant I saw it start to get out of hand I pleaded with the chairman of the day to end the debate.

Too late: the first fist had been thrown.

The first member to lose his cool, tried to win the argument with a poorly aimed punch, he was swiftly held from behind, and this was supposed to quell the violent outburst. It had the opposite effect because the person who should have received the incoming punch decided to hit the man who was being held from behind. Very gallant indeed!

From there on in it was a terrible fiasco, you have to appreciate it was a family gathering as it is to this day, and you do not want your families to see such ugly behaviour.

At least six or seven so-called men were involved in the mayhem all of which I hope to this day are thoroughly ashamed of themselves. I walked out well before the last punch was thrown.

18

By the way, the other point in question was the granting of too many honouree Memberships. That thankfully did not receive the same attention.

The Monthly Sunday meetings after that very sad, sorry fistfight never really seemed the same. People were apprehensive about bringing up points that they thought could or would cause violence to erupt again. It was a very long time before the membership at floor level had the confidence to air emotive subjects.

The Club now needed something to focus on that was away from the poison chalice of the CB. Extending our FUN DAY to three or at the very least two and a bit, days had been discussed many times before.

COUNTRY WEEKENDS

What we decided to do was combine the ever-popular fun day and truck show with a country music weekend.
Not content with that we would advertise it to incorporate a caravan and camping holiday weekend. Add that to two days clay shooting all the usual things we had done at the three previous fun days and chuck in a massive beer tent we could not lose!
Ha, how wrong could one be!

The task ahead was monstrous; we knew full well we were able to make the weekend a success: what we had not bargained for was the fact that not everybody can handle other people's money.
The first Country Weekend was a resounding and not too surprisingly a success. I was not privilege at the time to know the exact turnover but I knew the sum would be quite considerable. We are after all talking many thousands of pounds. Just to give you a rough idea of the kind of figures we are talking about, I was heavily into clay pigeon shooting and with the help of Mary a good friend Steven Dreary and his Wife Carol, we ran a two-day shoot. That shoot alone returned a clear profit of £700 per day.

We as the ECT ran two Country Weekends, the reasons for running only two of what would appear to be very profitable weekends, will become apparent as the story unfolds. We as organizers and small time entrepreneurs were getting smarter all the time, we could see what would make money what the punter wanted and how much to charge. We had people approaching us all year long wanting to have a piece of the action. Most of them were given a pitch as long as it did not interfere with any of our own enterprises.

One such attraction was an all female mud-wrestling troupe. They were, however, no ordinary mud wrestlers; half way through the bout, it was part of the act to completely strip your opponent.
My eyes never recovered from trying to see the bits that were not covered in thick mud. I know. So I am pervy, who isn't?

The final bout involved any member of the massed audience being invited to take part. I still have the photographs of a well-known surviving member's attempt at disrobing one of the very well equipped lady wrestlers. He lost more than his dignity, Andy Tait was never a shrinking violet, but he certainly took on more than he had bargained for with that lot.

While researching stories about the club from older members, I was told by Andy of his antics in the mud wrestling pit and what happened after the bout of mud wrestling. His story goes, apparently, there was only one shower at the event, and to stop the mud caking on too hard it had to be washed off pronto. Our man tells me he had no choice other than to get into the shower with the two girls he had just been assaulted by (likely story). After about an hour, he came out of the shower where he found his wife waiting for him with a towel. You will have to imagine the look on Andy's face, priceless.

That unfortunately was about all I can tell you about the good parts of our, and I will emphasize OUR, Country Weekend.

As I promised this is to be a true account of the history of the ECT as I saw it. If anybody wishes to refute the claims made here or put their case forward then they can be my guest. The next paragraph will shock all of you who are decent charitable people. Those with a guilty conscience should read no further.

A considerable amount of money was raised at our events the Country Weekend was obviously a little gold mine, and that was the main reason it was stolen from us. I will explain that unsavoury statement later on in this story.

I will now come to the previous statement I made about some people not being very good with other people's money. The last Country Weekend turned in a massive **loss** of £1200. Why? How? Surely, it could not be possible, as I said earlier my own clay shoot raised £1400 over the two days.

An inquest was duly held, questions were asked, and people were quizzed. No one came up with reasons that I could understand. I like many other people had a pretty good idea what happened to the missing funds. That and the way some people orchestrated the break-up of the East Coast Truckers leaves a very bad taste right up to this present day.

We had now started our sixth year, yet there is more to come before we go on to the very unpleasant story of the break up. First I must tell you more about the good times, the pleasant times and the times when the people you meet never leave your memory, also some of the more unsavoury and nasty pieces of work that have crossed the threshold of the ECT.

WESTWARD HO.

We, as one of the very first CB stroke Truckers Clubs that were springing up all over the British Isles, were quite rightly in communication with other clubs. One such club was The SOUTHWEST TRUCKERS CLUB, which like us is surprisingly still there to this day. There was also the A1 TRUCKERS CLUB the GEORDIE TRUCKERS CLUB and much later the LADY TRUCKERS CLUB. There were very many others but most of them came and went quicker than cheap diesel.

The club we struck up a very good alliance with was The South West Truckers Club. The bond of friendship was so strong that they arranged and organized a complete weekend down in Cheddar Gorge for all our members. That weekend will never leave my memory nor will it leave many others, some are still with the club to this day. This is their Story or rather nightmare.

I can vividly recall the weekend with a shudder and an affectionate tear like it was yesterday, most of the story will have you wondering if it really happened, believe me as sure as the pope wears a silly hat, it happened.

The plans were laid down as usual at the previous meeting. It was to be a two point meeting place; one at the now defunct Tuckswood Pub, the other out at the White Lodge Attleborough.
First problem, most of us were camping for the weekend but four or five of the better off and wimpish members had Wobble Boxes (caravans). The posh members arrived at the Tuckswood, duly waited four seconds and then went off without waiting for the poor people.

21

When the others arrived, they did not know that several had already left, so they waited and waited and waited. In the end, they decided to set off without the posh people not knowing that they had already gone: recipe for a row later I hear you thinking! By this time, they were now well and truly behind schedule, so the leader of the expedition stepped on the gas, as he did not want to miss the group that was leaving from the White Lodge.

We are talking about a long while before the Attleborough bypass was built here! On his approach to the White Lodge he apparently braked a little harder than the following car would have liked, we are talking a long while before ABS! That car in turn braked even harder than the first one and so on.

I believe you should have a good idea in your mind's eye what happened next. When I arrived with my group, the A11 looked the Road to Basra! Various parts of metal, glass and plastic littered the tarmac, a car was untidily parked here; another one there. After the obvious question about any injuries, I, in a rather agitated way, ask what had happened.

There were seven cars and one hundred and seven excuses! Professional drivers? Pa!

Four of the damaged cars with their respective occupants thought it would be prudent to write off the weekend (along with their cars), and go back home. The others bless them patched their wrecks up with tape and string and decided to go for it.

Now while most of the remaining cars looked a little sorry to say the least, one of them, well you would not believe it if you had been there, would not look out of place at Caister Stock Car Circuit, on any Sunday afternoon. It had started life as a rather smart MK4 Cortina

By now it was a good two to three feet shorter, all the crafted carefully by Ford glass had been replaced with cellophane and plastic bags. To be quite honest it was a disgrace, but the owner, Mr. Peter Wright, a.k.a. Eastern Cruiser, was determined to continue with his weekend. You could not fault the boy.

Incidentally he had inadvertently only insured his pride and joy third party and was seen parading around in his stock car for several months after that fateful afternoon. People rightly gave him a wide berth. They thought he was mad and bad. They were not all wrong!

But back to our journey:

We were now about three hours behind our military style plan, we were supposed to rendezvous with a delegation from the SOUTH WEST

22

TRUCKERS at a service area on the south bound M5.They had quite understandably thought we were not coming, (Oh for a mobile phone in those days) and by now were well into a booze up with the posh lot with the wobble boxes.

When we finally arrived at the campsite it was pitch dark, the restaurant booked for us had packed it in for the evening. This was getting worse by the minute, you will have to appreciate that back in those days my now big strapping sons were a pain in the backside back seat load of ankle biters. If they ask me one more time "Are we there yet dad?" or "I want a Wee Wee", I don't think I would have been responsible for my actions.

Everybody was getting tetchy we were hungry, tired and still had a flipping tent to erect.

True to form and when you are surrounded by the kind a characters that this industry spawns, it was only a matter of time before my knees would buckle due to an uncontrollable belly laugh.

Andy Tait had treated his young family to a long weekend but was too tight to buy his own tent, so he had scrounged one from some mate of his. This mate must have hated his guts; Andy diligently parked his car on a good solid high plot, just like the book tell you, opened his boot and proceeded to remove the mouldiest, mildewed bag you would ever see.

Watched keenly by his wife, he undid the suspicious looking apology for a tent, lined up and counted all the poles, positioned his ground sheet and finally unrolled the tent.

I do not think I will ever hear such foul language from such an innocent looking women again. She very nearly took his head off with the torrent of abuse. I will not and dare not repeat half of the words; we want this to be a family book.

Whatever was wrong I hear you and half of Somerset ask. On unrolling the tent, it became apparent that the last user had put it away wet. That in turn had left old Mother Nature and Mr. Mildew to reduce twenty square feet of canvas to little more than a shirt for a dwarf; it had more holes than Bin Laden's Caves.

My tent, along with most of the others went up quicker than a rocket leaving Cape Canaveral. Well we wanted to get up the pub didn't we!

If you have never experienced a full English breakfast cooked in the open air beside a tent, you ain't lived. The smell, not to mention the taste is something else. Stumbling out from under canvas on a summer morning, in that paradise of counties, to the smell of bacon, eggs,

23

mushrooms and thickly buttered toast, just somehow made the previous days debacle seem a million miles away.

The good people of the South West Truckers had arranged for us to play a game of footy against their finest players. The game soon turned into one great big make your rules up as you go along game. If you have seen Disney's Jungle Book and the footy match in that film, you should have a rough idea how ours was developing.

Did we win? You bet.

Diverting to another point, if ever we undertook a challenge in Norfolk, or anywhere else for that matter, we hardly ever lost. In the heydays of the club, people were reluctant to compete in any type of competition if they had a notion that the famous East Coast Truckers were coming. I must admit we were good.

Any way back to Somerset, a referee had been enlisted to see fair play. Half way through the first half, he went home. Why no one ever found out but I don't think he had seen our rulebook. Never mind, we won.

After the footy, they challenged us to a cross between a cricket and a rounders game. They had the advantage of knowing how to play or cheat at this one. We still thrashed them.

That evening saw us all sitting around and generally getting to know one another and obviously swapping trucking tales and yarns.

Their final challenge was a scrumpy drinking competition; I will tell you now they thrashed us something rotten on this one.

Devon is the natural home of what Jethro calls falling down water, to you and me scrumpy but no ordinary scrumpy given to the big Jessies that come down from the big cities. This stuff they gave us should not be allowed any where near living mortals.

I swear if you drunk that stuff and died the next day the undertaker would not need to fill you up with formaldehyde. The effect it had on me was much the same as the other poor innocents. I was in full control of my head and my thoughts but the connection between my brain and my body had been severed. I wanted my legs to go that way but my legs would just do their own thing. I went to stand up, I fell down, if you moved your arm, you had no idea where it would go or what it would do. Even the simple task of going to the toilet made the brain shudder at the consequences.

I fell into bed that night with the notion that my man hood was huge and I could make any women go weak at the very thought of it, I was duly informed that it was not huge and it certainly was not hard. Can't win them all can you!

24

Sadly the morning after the slaughtering we received at the hands of the scrumpy heads, saw us packing up to leave. We would have just enough time before the journey home to sample the delights of the near by Cheddar Gorge. If you have not been, it is well worth a visit, the narrow High Street winds its way up though the gorge flanked on either side with pretty shops selling all the usual touristy wares. There are some very good restaurants, lively pubs and a famous scrumpy house.

Back at the campsite, our hosts were assembled and ready to wave us off and you guessed they could not put enough emphasis on how safely we should drive. What on earth were they dribbling on about? We were with some of the best pilots that were ever born!

Oh yes I remember.

After much hugging, hand shaking kisses and cuddles, we were on our way. I will always be a sentimentalist and I must admit it was hard to ignore the lump in your throat or the tiny bit of moisture in your eye.

These total strangers had made us feel so special and had worked so hard to give us a wonderful time. However, would we return their kindness?

The drive home was completed without drama. My family was I guess much like all of our other travelling friends, reminiscing about the hilarious events that we had experienced that weekend.

We arrived home late and I fell into bed that night totally knackered, my darling wife and lovely kids were by now well asleep, it took all of my self-control to stop my silent snigger turning into a belly laugh. I had just remembered as we drove off the camp site in Devon, now so far away, looking at the assortment of aluminium poles and remnants of what was once a family tent, sticking quite sadly out of the waste skip. What a weekend!

THE MEDIA.

As any kind of club committee member will quite openly confirm, being elected to help with the running and day-to-day planning of a club is a thankless, unpaid but nevertheless rewarding task. My pleasure certainly came from helping with any success the club enjoyed.

Most of what was attempted by us turned into a well-performed event, even the fateful weekend in the West Country could only be described with affection because we all had such a wonderful time. We were really gelling as a club. We were also forming good relationships with our fellow members, and some of the friendships are still good to this day. At that time, even I had no doubt we would get larger and more powerful and an alternative to the now very unpopular Trade Unions.

Numerous organizations and clubs constantly approached us, either to help in a charitable way or to give advice relating to a road haulage matter. The local press, television and radio stations were very often contacting one of our committee for an in depth interview or to solve a technical problem. So when a request came to us from a television station in London, we leapt at the chance to give our all.

The television station in question was a new one to us simple country folk called TV AM. A very nice man, who I can only remember as James, spoke to me on the telephone in what I can only describe as a very camp voice. When we eventually met him my first assumption was a little unfair, because he turned out to be thoroughly decent and polite, much the same as many other programme producers we came to know over the next sixteen years.

The conversation on the telephone went roughly like this, "Hi Glenn my name is James and I have been commissioned to produce a short film about you butch rugged truckers". I could tell by the shake in his voice he was beside himself with excitement at the prospect of such close quarters contact with the type of people he had only read about.

Whatever did he expect? Our club had no one who looked even remotely liked Kris Kristofferson, we had no Love Machine and none of the wives would pass for Ali McGraw. We did have a few Dirty Lyle look-alikes though. (All of these characters featured in the classic movie "Convoy", it had the dubious distinction of being the only story ever based on a song. I highly recommend you dig it out of one of the second hand video shops. If our story is amusing you, you will love Convoy.)

After our initial conversation, he left me in the capable hands of his personal assistant and researcher. She was a tiny women and equally as bossy as her governor, whom I instantly liked even though at that time we had yet to meet face to face. They needed us to find a suitable location where they could get young children to ask a group of trucker's questions about the trucks and the life style of us truckers. They also needed a small number of trucks not only for background but also for action shots!

This was to be my first introduction to the making of a film or television programme, I will try not to boast too much, but we have over the years featured in very many such edits and programmes.

The whole process is a long drawn out affair involving an unimaginative number of people, and culminates at the end of a lot of hard work to only a few minutes of a film.

If I could have my life over again, 'would I take the path of a trucker again', is a question I have been asked many times. Not a sodden chance, I am coming back as a Television Producer.

The venue I found for the location was the old Enterprise Café on the A45 that is now the A428. I know. Why can't they just leave things alone? (Note: The Enterprise is now a housing estate.)

I must just digress here for a moment to tell you of an amusing tale concerning the Enterprise. The owner and manager was a charming likable fellow who ran a good café supplying good wholesome food to hundreds of truckers every day. The café had been there for as long as I could remember, it employed many local people and many catering suppliers made a good living from it.

Then along came some dickhead from the area food health department with the new guidelines that were drawn up by some Johnny Foreigner sitting on his big fat rear end in Brussels.

The said guidelines would have seen our very nice café owner ripping out his very clean kitchen to replace it with one that would cost about the same as the national dept of a small country.

What could the poor man do? He closed the café and installed a mobile tea stall right behind it. That is what you call EU intervention. Not wanting to sound too jingoistic but my father made a comment many years ago about fighting in two world wars to keep England free, then we go and give it to them anyway.

Once again, the truckers get the worst end of the deal.

Anyway, let us get back to James. Mary and I with our two eldest sons in tow made our way to the Enterprise Café one Saturday morning. We were all travelling in my truck of the day, which was a Scania LB141, my pride and joy.

Two other members and their children accompanied us. When we arrived another trucker who had been invited by Scania Varbis, who were to sponsor the film, joined us.

James and his crew arrived as we were finishing our forth mug of tea.

James was dressed in a full-length black leather designer coat; he had his hair similar to Michael Jackson's. You could tell he was not hard up for a few bob. In spite of his lardy-dah looks and the fact we were from different worlds I liked him. He had a genuine interest in how I earned a living and I think our banter and anecdotes amused him immensely.

The camera and sound crew were equally pleasant chaps and we all seem to hit it off quite nicely.

The café closed at 12 o'clock on Saturdays so it was decided we would plan the film and then execute it after 12 o'clock. At the planning and discussion stage, I only being a thick trucker feared asking a question that had been puzzling me since the second mug of tea. Where were the children that were to ask the truckers the searching questions?

Eventually I summoned the courage to ask.

You could see blood drain even from James very brown face, "Oh my god, Oh my god, Oh my god," was all James could say, yes James had lost it. They, the professionals had forgotten to bring the children.

When the programme finally went out several weeks later, I would not imagine anybody other than our own families knew that all the children asking the questions were indeed our own.

I still have a copy of the film and at times of great nostalgia; I get it out of its dusty box and have a chuckle. It lasts all of four long minutes.

It consumed 9 hours of our time not including the journey to and from Cambridge.

We were paid handsomely for the day, James bought us all lunch. Oh and we got a lovely letter of thanks.

I must admit I thoroughly enjoyed the experience, as I say next time a Producer I will be.

At about the time of the Tele fame, we were approached by a new truckers magazine called Truck and Driver.

The editor wanted to write an article depicting the plight of the modern trucker, who better to ask than the East Coast Truckers?

The magazine had had many stories of adverse treatment of truckers from various sources and would like our views to the same.

I will explain much later in this book about our bond with Norfolk Police but at that time, there was much bad felling regards the attitude to truckers by all the enforcement agencies including the Police.

Joe Public again features quite predominantly here regarding bad attitude to truckers as well.

Anyway the editor sent a reporter and a photographer up from London to meet with us.

We as a committee gave a fairly articulate responsible account of how we saw things, we let them take as many photos as they needed and we aired a few grievances. One of our many gripes that still exist to this day was given extensive coverage in the article to be published.

Joe Public will not be aware of the fact that even though many factories and distribution warehouses would close if it not for the arrival of one of our trucks, our truck drivers are not allowed to use any of the facilities enjoyed by the employees of the recipient firm. We are expected to sit in our cabs for however long it may take to unload the truck, without any toilet or refreshment facilities.

The better ones, I will use that term loosely, install a portaloo and a tea machine. Men with dark skins were treated better in the deep south of America.

The sting in the tale of this little excursion into the realms of the media would beggar belief. The editor of the afore-mentioned publication thought it would be a good idea to send along a photographer. His intention was to take some shoots of members with their respective trucks. The meet was to take place at my home at Attleborough. About six trucks had been parked outside my house for less than the time it takes to make a cup of tea, when up turns the local panda car with its obvious cargo.

ALLO! ALLO! ALLO! What's going on 'ere then? Yes, it really did happen just like that.

One of my lovely neighbours, whom obviously, had never had anything delivered by truck, took great exception to all these trucks being parked on his road! So the good citizen rang the police to complain. Makes good copy, yes!

While I have always tried to champion the truckers cause, I was unaware of the twist of fortune that getting too involved in the harder and political side of trucking was to bring. That's a longer story again I will eventually come to.

I suppose it is only fair to give you a better insight into what made us the club and its member's tick.

Truck drivers are unique and about as diverse as any type of professional you will find. A BBC television producer, who once spent three days with me in my truck to research yet another programme, likened us to the pilot of an airliner. Making a similarity to the skill and responsibility, I would not go quite that far but I got his drift.

The very nature of the job demands that you have to work very long hours; be away from your family for most of the week, and you have to work and survive on your own initiative. You will also experience long periods of loneliness and isolation. If something goes wrong at home, you are, more often than not, too far away to be able to do anything about the impending problem. Add that to the general way you are perceived and treated and you can then see where the thirst for fun and hell raising is fostered.

It would be quite wrong to say there is a typical trucker, although we have all seen the stereo type, one of our later television programmes, featured a spoof send up of truck drivers eating hedgehog sandwiches.

The truck drivers we were involved with were a little easier to define, mainly because they were now joining the club not for the afore mentioned insurance against Busby but to let off steam and frustration, by helping others, and at the same time enjoy the company of like minded people.

Asked to describe the character and generalize the personalities I would say that they were nothing other than the salt of the earth. Their hearts were as big as the trucks they piloted, their energy and generosity had no bounds, these were the type of people with few exceptions you would always be proud to call friends.

ALL THINGS MUST PASS

Rumblings of impending troubled waters seemed to manifest itself with the dawn of every monthly club meeting. Although it was difficult to put a precise finger on exactly what would happen and when.

It seemed at this time it was only myself and one other committee member that were pulling in the same direction, but apart from the very nasty fracas a couple of years earlier not much would give people on the outside of the club much of a clue that anything was amiss.

If there was to be major problems in the club, I was not alone in thinking the trouble would stem from money and money alone.

A small clue to where the trouble would eventually come from emerged from one of our many committee meetings. We often met at a public house in Norwich. It was at one of these meetings that a so-called responsible person really got into a little paddy and chucked all of his toys out of the pram. He was ranting and raving, all because he was having difficulty in winning an argument about something not very important. I, and my confederate of the time, could see that the rant was being

30

Left:
The lead truck of the
first East Coast
Truckers convoy in
1986 approaching the
Blowfield flyover.

Below:
View from the cab of
the lead truck as the
first convoy heads
along the Golden
Mile of Great
Yarmouth in 1986.
(From Glenn D.
Johnson)

Clockwise from bottom left:1987Convoy at Pettits of Reedham, Police Escort of 1987, Sgt. Dick Howardthe first Norfolk Police assistant, The lead truck for the 1988 convoy.

(Supplied by Glenn Johnson.)

The 1993 Convoy at Great Yarmouth's Golden Mile. (From Nick Ireland)

The Children's Convoy in 1993 proceeding along Yarmouth's Golden Mile (Nick Ireland)

**More trucks at the Children's Convoy at Great Yarmouth in 1993.
(Nick Ireland)**

Peter Allard

Bottom: 1993 Convoy at Great Yarmouth (From Nick Ireland). Top: 1994
Convoy at Reedham. (From Peter Allard).

36

**The ninth East Coast Truckers at Reedham Riverside in 1994.
(From Peter Allard)**

37

East Coast Truckers Club on a boat trip. (Teresa Wilce)

purposefully orchestrated. I began to wonder why I was giving up my Saturday evenings to listen to this kind of childish behaviour.

All of these suspicions apart, we were still a very successful club. Up until the break-up during late1985 and early 1986, we were striving ahead with more and more adventurous and headline grabbing events.

By the time of the forth year of existence we had built up a fairly competent team of Tug of War. We challenged all comers and very rarely lost. We claim it was on the grounds of pure strength and strategy, others would say otherwise; jealousy is a wicked thing.

Along the same lines, we had developed a very good short distance truck pulling team. We competed for charity, as well as the usual fun that accompanied all of our endeavours.

We had regular bowling evenings; pub nights and a very ambitious clay pigeon shooting club had been formed. This clay pigeon club was funded by the ECT for the members of the club and their families; we had secured a small parcel of land from Billy Watling, we purchased some basic clay traps, and then summoned the help of keen members and we were away.

This offshoot of the ECT was a success from the start. After about three months of weekend shoots we had attracted inquires from other clay shooters about joining our club. If they were not bona fide holders of an HGV license they could not join the ECT, but we did allow them to shoot as guests of the club, for a small fee obviously.

The clay club was two years old, when the management of the nearby Lotus car factory approached us. They were very interested in sending members of their management team to shoot with us as a reward for their endeavours, a sort of corporate treat.

We quite rightly accepted their proposal, the first Saturday about eight people from Lotus came to shoot, and they were all impressed with the way we ran our club. The following meet saw nearly twenty shooters, along with their families and friends.

The clay club would continue for the next couple of years as an offshoot of the ECT. Eventually we noticed that very few actual ECT members were attending the shoots so I approached the committee about taking over the clay cub in its entirety. They agreed as long as the original investment the ECT made was compensated.

Mary and I, along with Steven and Carol Drewry, successfully ran the shoots for another five years. We eventually sold out to a neighbouring club because we no longer had the time to devote to the shoot and to our own business.

"All things come to pass" was a very good album by George Harrison and the title seemed to be the only way I can describe one of the two very dark chapters in the history of the ECT.

As described previously we as a club were doing very well on all fronts, I although having a rather pessimistic view of the way I feared the club would eventually fall on its own sword.

If I had seen it coming earlier, neither I nor anybody else could have prevented the following sad chapter, because it had quite obviously been contrived with much cunning for longer than we could have imagined.

This being the first of the two sad situations was very much like the second one, self-inflicted.

It is my belief that the first one was purely money driven, rather than political like the second.

Sadly, the club ended up with a badly bloodied nose, unlike the second one where I sustained a little more damage. Hind sight what a wonderful thing.

The Country Weekends were undoubtedly a resounding success; they commanded large sums of money and substantial media attention.

We had no idea at that time that some person or persons were interested in running our Country Weekend for financial gain. Nothing was ever proven and no fingers were ever to be pointed.

Although the whole story is somewhat hazy after all this time, I can recall quite vividly the main core of the scenario and the outcome.

The Country Weekends were held at Strumpshaw Hall. The owners of the hall had agreement with a privileged few members of the club that we the club, would donate a percentage of the takings to a charity of their choice, by way of a kind of rent.

Not all of the committee were privy to all of the details and consequently the last Country Weekend, which I stated earlier had made a massive loss, could not find the funds to meet the guarantees previously promised.

The owners of the venue although patient up to a point, were not long in making legal move overtures; worrying to say the least.

In all the time the club had been running this was the first time we had encountered an adverse and hostile atmosphere. Not to mention financial cramp.

We had gotten ourselves into a precarious situation and we had no idea of how to tackle it.

A hurried general meeting was held, with the intention of finding a way to stave off the legal action pending and the very bad publicity that would follow as surely as night follows day.

Most of the suggestions would have cost us more than we had any hope of covering financially.

So it was decided that if we wound up the East Coast Truckers Club, there would be little point of anybody mounting legal action against a defunct organization. So it was. A small ad was published in the local public notices column. The East Coast Truckers Club was now officially dead.

At the same time, it was deemed to start a new truckers club to be called the **EAST COAST TRUCKERS 86 CLUB**. To this day, I am not entirely certain we were bordering on the illegal, but it did work. To this day, we have never heard any more about the legal action threatened against the original club.

The first meeting of the newly formed, if somewhat fragmented club was held at the now gone Highway Café on the old A47, just opposite the entrance to the Norfolk Showground. Around fifty old members made an appearance.

Needless to say, I was there to offer my services to the new club and was duly invited to take up the mantle of Public Relations, a role I seemed to have done before.

I must admit that most of the new committee was a revamp version of the old club with the noted exception of just two people.

These two ex members stated that they would not be joining the new club. They were apparently too busy organizing a Country Music Weekend at Strumpshaw Hall. Enough said!

HERALD OF FREE ENTERPRISE.

Jumping forward here to 1987 will give a little bit better insight to how the Children's Convoy and eventually the East Coast Truckers Charity were destined to be.

One of the biggest deeds of the fragmented, but newly formed club was brought about purely through tragedy.

One dark night on March the 6th 1987, a cross channel ferry had just completed its loading of cars and trucks at the port of Zeebrugge, Belgium. During the process of putting to sea a combination of freak circumstances caused the whole vessel to Capsize and sink, along with its cargo of 80 crew, 459 passengers, 81 cars, 3 buses, and 47 trucks.

As you would expect a public enquiry was held and its findings were to shock and dumfound many people, as well as myself. We who used these ferries thought we were safe and as safe as houses.

At the public enquiry, we learned that it was common practice among all ferry operators to close the outer bow doors and make ready for sea while the vessel was leaving the sanctuary of the inner harbour. The enquiry was also told that the process was always completed before the ferry made open water.

This was pure and simply a way of turning the vessel around in ever quicker times.

The company, as well as the crew, were found to be at fault for the disaster of the "HERALD OF FREE ENTERPRISE".

As most of you will have travelled at some time on these ever-growing ferries, you will understand the horror of the events surrounding that fateful evening.

Because of the industry, we operate in; we are quite used to driving aboard these large vessels without a moment's thought about the consequences of the thing ever falling over.

If you were not on this vessel this fateful evening, you can only imagine with terror what did happen.

Firstly, the ship keeled over and sank in thankfully shallow water. The enquiry was told that the whole process of keeling over and sinking took seconds rather than minutes. Anyone who survived had to first endure the initial shock of impending disaster. If they survived the drop to the bottom of what became the floor instead of a bulkhead, they then had to dodge other people on their way down from what was now a very great height (these ferries are over two hundred feet wide) as well as all the un-fixed fitting and personal effects.

Combine this with cold deep water filling the inside of the vessel and all the lights going out, add disorientation and panic and now you will have some idea of the turmoil and tremor the survivors experienced

The people who were on the passenger decks had a fairer chance of survival than the truckers who were still on the car decks. It is hard to dodge a truck falling from that height. We can only hope and pray they met their ends very quickly.

A sad total of 150 passengers and 38 crew lost their lives. Many others were seriously injured.

Several recommendations were made and implemented at the Public Enquiry; some of the main points were that all passengers would vacate the car decks before sailing.

The Captain would have the use of CCTV and that all doors would be closed and sealed before the vessel moved from its moorings.

The ECT sprang into action within hours of the sinking. One of our members had been in contact with a group who had identified themselves as the fundraisers and organizers of the disaster fund set up for the Herald of Free Enterprise.

Within days, the disaster fund trustees had made a few inquiries about our mettle and decided to make us sole agents for the raising of money in the Norfolk area. That is to say, if you could or did not want to send your donation to the fund or put it in the bank, you could give it to us knowing that it would reach its chosen destination.

The very next Saturday we had gained permission from the City of Norwich street collections department to collect funds in Gentleman's Walk. An event we still attend although now for our own charity.

We were loaned two top of the range super trucks from DUFFIELDS OF EAST ANGLIA. (This local Volvo dealer was another big contributor to the pinnacle of all our achievements THE EAST COAST TRUCKERS CHILDREN'S CONVOY.) Duffields were always and to this day a very good friends and accomplices of the ECT.

We started our street collection for the disaster at about 10am on the Saturday morning and at 5pm that evening people were still pushing money at us.

In actual fact when word got around people were travelling into the city centre with sole intention of giving us their donation.

We also hastily put together a benefit dance at the Talk nightclub. This was an area where we knew we could only shine; some of our best organizers pulled together for what would become a very emotional and memorable evening.

The Lord Mayor of Norwich attended the dance and if nothing else, it gave the evening credence.

When the fund was eventually wound down, we had collected the staggering sum of £12,500: not bad, even by our perfectionist standards. You can do a load of good with money like that.

Bearing in mind all of the victims, especially truckers, lost everything they had with them on that fateful evening.

One poor trucker who resided not too far from our Norwich base made an innocent request to us, for a small sum of money to replace all the sleeping and personal gear he had lost on the vessel.

We duly contacted the fund organizers about the said request. Their reply furthered my beliefs about charity at home and all that.

Their memo read:

"Dear Sirs

Further to your enquiry about Mr. X, and his unfortunate loss aboard the Herald of Free Enterprise. We as trustees of the charity have sole discretion as to how the funds are to be allocated and to whom. If Mr. X contacts us in the first instant, we will attend to his request in good time."

The poor trucker wanted his sleeping bag and personal effects now. I am sure if just one of those generous Norwich citizens had seen that memo they would have demanded their money back. I would have. Did I say something earlier about doing a lot of good with that kind of money? You could not make the next bit up in a hundred years.

Here we were with a small fortune collected for distressed and needy people, given very generously by well-intentioned people. Could we give it away? Could we hell as like! We would have had more luck getting the pope to wear a condom.

The more we tried to locate the trustees of the fund the more we came up against a brick wall. Here we are with over £12,000 we seemed to be stuck with. It would be three long years before we would finally pass on the money to the so-called disaster fund.

My theory of charity begins at home is getting stronger.

Nevertheless even that slight blip on the part of our judgment would help in years to come, when we embarked on our most famous and highly prestigious event.

44

You might say someone was preparing us for greater things!

The social side to the club was still as buoyant as ever. We were forever attempting new ways to keep the enthusiasm for fun alive and kicking. As well as the Clay Shooting, we were entertaining our members and their families with ever more and varied events. At the last dinner dance as the original ECT, we had succeeded in selling more than three hundred tickets so the proof was there for all to see that even in the guise of a new club, we were a long way from being just another flash in the pan club. In spite of the break up, we were still going strong.

We had even hired a complete cinema for a private showing of the by now cult classic film, 'Convoy'. Supporting the main feature was a couple of films not readily known, but very good, if you are a bit of a truck freak. I can recall them to be 'Duel' with Dennis Weaver and a very obscure film called 'White Line Fever'.

Another Saturday night special was, believe it or not, Wine and Cheese Evenings.

THE FIRST CONVOY.

Only a few weeks of the newly formed club had passed, when all of a sudden I realized that for the first time in six years we as a club, and me as a family man, because of the missing Country Weekend, had no plans for the fast approaching August Bank Holliday.

What the hell, let's just chuck the kids in the car and clear off to a Zoo or something, or may be sit in the garden with me feet up.

Not this stupid individual.

Where I first got the idea it is hard to say, I do not think the whole idea came in one go, it kind of crept up on me wrestled me to the floor, then beat me into submission.

We had of course the organizational skills, we had a good rapport with the traffic police, remember the gorilla! We had trucks; we had access to directors and managers of local businesses, we had money. We had also, over the period of the last few years, helped a local handicapped Children's Home with a multitude of tasks and favours. Put them all into a great big mixing bowl, hold your ears here comes **THE EAST COAST TRUCKERS CHILDREN'S CONVOY.**

45

Repton House is situated just off St Faith's Road on the outskirts of Norwich, located in a very pretty but typical English suburb. You would never have considered it typical on Sunday August 29th 1986!

Jammed into its very small cull de sac were 22 highly polished trucks along with their equally polished owners and families.

I had along with Mary visited the Handicapped home on numerous occasions, so when we approached the caretakers of the home about our intended day out for the children who reside there, they were more than helpful.

Our first visit some weeks earlier was to ascertain what children we would be able to accommodate on the trip. Even way back then most of the membership piloted the so-called super trucks; most of them are a good climb of about 6 feet from the ground to the seating.

Already we could see that not every child would be suitable.
We made a pact then that we would move every obstacle possible in order that very few children would be deemed unsuitable. That rule still holds, right up to this present day.

I had also visited every resident of the nearby houses seeking their permission and support for the convoy; to their credit, they agreed and also came out to support us on the day.
We had notified the police well in advance of how we would conduct ourselves and where we were going, complete with a timetable.
We at the same time had asked for their help.

The local Volvo dealer had been approached, to give what ever they could by way of a small gift for our guests for the day.
DUFFIELDS OF EAST ANGLIA, Volvo Truck Dealers, were by definition our first ever sponsors. NEVILLE LOOME was the sales manager for Duffields and along with a younger member of his team helped enormously in our quest to make these young charges of ours feel very special.

As a matter of interest, that younger member of Neville's team was TONY SADDLER who went on to become managing director of the whole Duffields group some years later.
I had in the weeks leading up to our convoy dwelled on where it would be best to take the children for the day.

A new venue had just been opened at Lowestoft. PLEASUREWOOD HILLS was perfect. It was not to far away, it had large parking facilities and there was something there for everybody.

I had negotiated a free entrance for the truck driver and his handicapped child, and a concessionary price for every one else.

To fill the day it was planned to take the children to a tea party at Great Yarmouth, to be totally accurate we actually took the children to COBHOLM COMMUNITY CENTRE, which was run by my mother Doreen and her team of helpers. Directly after this we would take the children home to Norwich via Great Yarmouth's GOLDEN MILE.

Later I will give a better insight to the people of Cobholm, as the place and the people were quite unique and instrumental to the fame of the convoy.

At this time, it would be rather rude not to mention that the first person on the out side of the club to really shine with devotion and kindness was ironically my mum, MRS. DOREEN JOHNSON.

My mum had been tirelessly working to improve the local community centre, situated just across the road from where she lived with my father. When I suggested bringing the trucks to Cobholm, she went straight into top gear.

They, as she and her merry band of helpers did for the next thirteen years, made the day what it was.

Over the years there have been very many Doreen's, I will try to name check, as many as I can, but there will obviously be people that have slipped my mind. Please except my profound apology if you are one of these kind and godly people.

So the theme was set, we had assembled at 8 o'clock; been greeted by the Sheriff of Norwich, a very kindly lady, along with her husband. We loaded up our precious cargo and were ready for the off at 10oclock sharp.

At precisely 9.45am our requested police help turned up; one traffic patrol car with one police officer. Great! He would take us to Pleasurewood Hills, where upon he informed me that after that, we were on our own.

Charming! Twenty-two trucks, twenty-two handicapped children and all our families would now be my responsibility. I got them there. I now had to get them all home and safely!

But first let us party, we had arranged with the managers of Pleasurewood Hills to set aside a private area where we could have a picnic. They, as with all our other requests, agreed. Mary, along with the help of three very helpful local girls, spent the whole of Saturday evening making sandwiches and rolls for every body on the convoy. We had persuaded shopkeepers wherever we could to donate a cake here and a biscuit there.

Every body was enjoying the day but there was more to come yet. At 3o'clock we loaded up the trucks again to make our way to Cobholm. Now as I said here we were with 22 trucks and no police escort back to Great Yarmouth. Necessity is the mother of invention, and we proved it to be very true.

When we approached the first roundabout on our way back to Great Yarmouth, the truck directly behind me, me being the lead truck, peeled off to cover the entrance to the roundabout, thus making sure that the convoy stayed together. Clever clogs, eh! Not entirely sure if we were not breaking the law, but it had the desired effect. We managed to keep our very good-looking convoy in one piece.

When all the trucks had cleared the roundabout the truck acting as block would take up his place at the back of the convoy. That is pretty much the way it was all the way home.

When we arrived at Cobholm, we had arranged to park the trucks into the local schools playground. This in itself would have been a good entry for Record Breakers!

My mum along with all her helpers made all of our guests more than welcome. They provided music and various other forms of entertainment. Over the years, it became more and more ambitious, with all of us taking part.

I had decided very early on in the planning stages of the convoy, that one part of the day should be devoted to a trip a long Great Yarmouth's Golden Mile. So it was; as soon as we had loaded up our trucks at Cobholm we were off along the sea front. Our intention was to show the children the whole length of the Golden Mile, not releasing that we would have quite an impact on the visitors to the attraction.

We immediately realized we were on to a winner with this part of the convoy. We brought the sea front to a complete standstill both on and off the road, bearing in mind this was the first ever convoy and nobody had prior warning that we were coming. There was calls coming from the back end of the convoy saying, "Lets do it all again".

I had other pressing things on my mind; I still had to get this 22 truck convoy home to Norwich and without any incidents.
We arrived back at Repton House at exactly the time we had stated on the timetable. So here we are back at Repton House, there was quite a good

feeling amongst all of the participants, we were high on euphoria and over whelmed by everybody's response.

One other thing everybody had noticed, we were all thoroughly knackered. I can quite honestly say that taking part in the East Coast Truckers Children's Convoy was as hard as a journey to Aberdeen and back.

The whole of the areas residents had turned out to wave, clap and cheer us home. That's when I had my first real feelings of satisfaction and that was when I thought all the preparation had been worthwhile, and I realized this was too good to be just a one off. We would have to do it again.

The Children's Convoy was never intended to be an annual affair. We had a bank holiday with a gapping hole in it. We, as a club, were desperate to run an event similar to the one that was stolen from us. That was what we had become very good at. Could we find something as good as the Country Weekend?

As I noted earlier the convoy never came to me in all one big flash, once the seed was sown it started to gel all of its own accord, so to speak.

I had quite obviously notified our intended convoy to the local papers. They in turn decided to run a small article on us and the convoy. The article was published with the astonishing revelation that we were not the first people in the Norfolk area to run a charity convoy.

The first one, although not exactly the same as ours, bore similarities that were unbelievable.

The first convoy consisted of a few coaches, trucks and an assortment of other vehicles; they were like our own trucks loaned quite generously by local firms, and people who had given up their day off drove them. They loaded them up with as many children as they could and took them all out on a picnic to a large park near Guist.

The main organizer of this original children's day out, got in touch with me and we had a very informative conversation.

This first children's convoy took place during 1930 and 1945. So although we lay claim to being the first convoy of its kind, it was not technically so.

The London Taxi Drivers Outing also takes children out for the day to Southend. Nevertheless, ours is still unique, our format has been the same since day one and while I am in the chair, it will not change.

At the time of planning our second convoy, I felt that although we were not promised any help from the authorities, we had to look as professional as we possibly could. I had run the route we would take many times, both in my car and in my truck. That is why in those days our timing was faultless, I had made sure everywhere we went local people had been notified, so as not to cause too much unfavourable reactions.

It was also an early rule that the trucks would be highly polished and fit for any ministry inspection.

That is basically how the convoy stayed for the first 4 years.

The first four convoys were run by Mary and I, lock, stock and barrel; we had very little outside help as most of the committee was over stretched doing other things. With the exception of Sheila and Ray Sarsby coming to our rescue regards finding suitable children, it was very much a family and very close friend's affair

But would we, and could we, do it again? At the September's meeting, it has always been the day to have an inquest into the happenings of the convoy. It was my original intention to run the convoy only once.

At the September meeting, the millstone was being fastened to the chain that would eventually be tied to my neck.

What could I do? Everybody was still on a high, everybody congratulated me on a wonderful idea, and everyone was emphatic that we had to do it again.

What could I do? History was being made.

Apart from the convoy, we were still a very good social club and ever since the birth and rebirth of the East Coast Truckers, we have had a Christmas party for our own children. Every thing was funded by the club, unlike our own Dinner Dance, which had to return a profit.

The Christmas party as far as I can remember was mostly run at our base The Norfolk Dumpling, apart from the very few years we had our base at the Anglian Windows Social Club.

We had all the usual party things like mince pies and trifle; Father Christmas was the ultimate event, and there was always a variety of entertainment.

It was several years into the convoy years when it was decided to invite the children we had taken on the convoy to the Christmas party. That is why I can still remember with horror some parties having over 100 children running absolute riot. We must have been nuts!

The club was starting to forget the previous years black period, we were going ahead with all the usual entertainment, and somebody was always trying out new ways to encourage excitement and enthusiasm.

50

We were organizing quiz nights and on a few occasions we attempted a spoof 'Mr and Mrs Competition'.

There always seemed to be more going on than you could be at, but nevertheless most of the events were well attended.

POLICE INVOLVEMENT

I was by the end of April 1987, well into the setting up of our second convoy; part of that planning was to inform the police of our intentions regard the running of the convoy when Mary received a worrying call from the traffic department of the Norfolk Police. I feared the worst.

They wanted to interview the organizer of last year's convoy. Cripes! I thought they are going to block our convoy.

An Evil Kineval, or traffic motorcycle cop to you and me, pulled up in my driveway one May afternoon in 1987.A tall fellow hauled himself from the horizontally pistoned BMW. All in all a good six foot of police officer stood in my doorway. He removed his crash helmet to reveal a shock of red hair. "Hello Mr. Johnson, my name is Sergeant Dick Howard, may I come in?"

He explained to Mary and me that although there had been no complaints, as far as he was aware, and no problem with the running of our first convoy, he was a messenger from a higher authority that was expressing concerns on the safety aspect of the children's convoy. In a nutshell, his superiors had sent him to see if he could persuade us not to repeat our convoy this year.

After putting our case and telling him about the shabby way we had been treated as to our previous August Bank Holiday activities, Sergeant Howard said in a somewhat defeated tone, "Well my second set of instructions is this. In the event of you still insisting on running the convoy, can we the traffic department of the Norfolk Constabulary, over see the Queens Highway side of things and escort you for the whole day?" Music to my ears. Yes! By crikey! Yes! I would have been off my rocker to do anything other than agree.

This was the very approval we had been waiting for; this would be the making of the convoy as far as public acceptance.

This was the only way forward. We now had the official backing of the authorities; we had now made the jump to the big time, with still no idea of just how big it would one day be.

51

Dick, as I will now call him, was quite enthusiastic about the organizational side of the convoy as far as the police were concerned. He spent very many hours travelling the route we were to take ironing out any problems that I had not seen. That second convoy was the benchmark by which all other convoys would be run.

To this day, we are indebted to Sergeant Dick Howard.

Dick retired from the convoy and the police force in 1992, he is doing well and he still supports our and his convoy.

At the last convoy he over saw for us, we presented him with a cut glass model of a Harley Davidson. That is how you make a policeman weep.

THE EARLY CONVOYS.

The first convoy although a resounding success, lacked flair and polish, I do not mean the trucks, as far as most people were concerned the trucks were a picture of professional elegance. No, I mean the overall way the convoy was run, from the assembly point in the morning to the greeting of the parents and carers when we arrived home. I set to work finding ways we could improve without changing too much of the format.

First of all, the second years convoy doubled in size, we were fielding 46 trucks plus 2 support vehicles.

We would have to find a different venue to assemble on the Sunday morning, because last years 22 trucks only just squeezed into the Cul-De-Sac of Repton House.

I contacted the car parks department of Norwich City Hall.

They granted permission for us to use the large car park on Castle Plain; if you are familiar with Norwich, you will know that to be where there now stands the Castle Mall Shopping Precinct. By the way, I do not think they had any choice in granting my wishes, because I did notify the department that the Lord Mayor of Norwich would be there to greet the children and the truckers.

What a namedropper!

I had written to the Lord Mayors office, inviting him to be the guest of honour at the start of our convoy His secretary made a few inquiries as to our esteem. A few weeks later came the acceptance letter along with a short list of protocol.

We have never had a convoy leave Norwich since without the blessing of that much-esteemed person.

Now we were starting to shine.

The first convoys were by choice totally controlled and organized by Mary and I; we cadged help wherever we could, and it is fair to say we were never short of volunteers. The first people to offer their services were known to most of the local truckers as the "Three Nuns". I mean this in the nicest way possible, but how they got that pet name, I will never know. They were three of the most helpful and pleasant young girls you would wish to find.

In the first 4 or 5 convoys, Mary and I could not have performed the tasks of the day without Anetta and Tracy Lancaster and Carol Spalding.

We, as a thank you to all the drivers and their families, provided every body on the convoy with a picnic lunch at our afternoon venue. I say afternoon venue because we would not always go to Pleasurewood Hills.

As you could imagine making a picnic lunch for nearly 200 people was quite a feat. The food was requisitioned from whatever source possible; the club would pay for the remainder.

Mary, with the Three Nuns help, spent all of the Saturday evening before the convoy making sandwiches and cakes. My job was to mark out where the trucks would assemble on the Sunday morning, and of course, I had to polish my own truck.

I would get in at about 10 pm. I would run though the final plans for the day. Finally as a thank you to the girls and Mary I always came though the door with a liberal quantity of alcoholic beverages. Not a good idea considering the early start we had; what the hell!

The lead up to the convoy for myself these days is quite relaxed, in so much as now I have a team of well orchestrated people who know exactly what has to be done and when. In the early years my convoy organizing, much as today started way back in March. The police were my first contact, then the Lord Mayors office followed by our afternoon venue owners, possible sponsors and of course Mum.

Most of the trucks were donated and driven by club members, as with tradition we have always invited truckers from outside the club to guest for the day.

I have to this day, tried to guard this side of the convoy against the wrong kind of truck or person. A situation that has not always been popular, but at the end of the day the buck stops with me. The criteria and format built up over the years never happened by accident, as an example I do not regard 'Wendy Houses' as being suitable for our convoy.

(To define Wendy Houses, they are designed and built with the soul purpose of local delivery. Needless to say, they have very little space for a driver or any over night equipment he may need. Some transport operators purchase these Wendy Houses and put them to work on long distance and even continental haulage runs. A policy I have always criticized and always will.)

The first question I would ask a potential guest trucker would be what type of truck are you likely to field. If it was a Wendy House the application would be refused; mainly because the things are too cramped for the children and the other occupants, secondly they look a bit lame surrounded by proper premium trucks. If a member donated one of the so called Wendy Houses I had little choice in accepting the offer, but believe you me I did not like it one little bit. In addition, I certainly let my views be known.

This would be a good time in the story to talk about the four elements of the convoy. These are the trucks, the truckers, the children and finally the saints.

THE TRUCKS

At the time of writing, over 1700 trucks have carried more than 1700 children a total of 12000 miles since the convoy began. We have had many incidents, never had an accident or an injury, but we have had very many funny situations. I will come to some of them all at some stage. In the main, we have never lost a child or a truck. That is apart from Nicky my loyal number 2 breaking down on the morning of the convoy!

That is a record we did not come to by accident; forgive the pun. I have prided myself on selecting a format that would have us seen on the day of the convoy to be absolute professionals. The trucks must be presented clean, polished and roadworthy; there should be no bits hanging from the truck i.e. ropes, chains or spare parts. They will not be decorated in any way what so ever. All lights are to been seen to be working, and no more than 5 people are to be on board when the convoy sets off. To encourage the good appearance of the trucks and the convoy we always

Betty Tortice.

2011 Norfolk Gala Day   **Hutchinson**

conduct a very tongue in cheek competition. This competition is run throughout the day of the convoy, and three trophies are presented to the winners, at the end of day party. We try to keep this part as low key as possible but you would not believe the standard we have witnessed over the years.

56

With but a few exceptions the trucks are a credit to the drivers, the convoy and the trucking industry; something I am very proud of. There have however been a few rather embarrassing situations

One trucker turned up at the assembly point with a truck that had just come off night trunk; his excuse was the truck he had been promised failed to materialize. He was sent somewhere with a bucket and sponge and a few volunteers to help him get the truck into some kind of presentable condition.

Another amusing occurrence involved Chris Mullings, a very good member of the day; I received a rather distressed phone call on the morning of the convoy. The conversation went some thing like this "I am sorry I have had a bit of an accident". "Oh yes", was my rather curt reply. "Well what happened was", he continued, "I got up this morning, loaded up my truck with my bits and pieces for the day and thought I would warm the old girl up. Now as you know I live on a bit of a hill. When I was loading it up, I must have inadvertently knocked off the hand brake; the air was down so I would not have noticed. "The next thing I knew" said Chris "there was a knock on my door and a very irate neighbour asking me to get my great big truck out of his garden". "Is it all right if I still come?" asked Chris. What could I say; the poor chap was beside himself with embarrassment but did not want to let his child of the day down. An admirable attitude I have seen very many times.

(Note: Modern trucks have a safety feature that locks on the brakes in the event of the air pressure being too low, as the air pressure comes back to normal the brakes are automatically released, if the hand brake is in the off position, and you are on a hill, you and your truck are in the crap.)

He turned up at the departure point with a slightly battered truck but with a bit of help from the other truckers it did not look that bad.

Not quite as bad as the crimson complexion he wore for the rest of the day, you can just imagine the cruel quips.

We have had all kinds of problems with donated trucks leading up to the convoy, a good friend decided to up end his only days before one convoy, others have suffered various serious break downs and accidents. Something I try to cater for so as to not disappoint any of our children guests. One such incident I recall was a truck breaking down on the morning of the convoy and not making an appearance, the cheeky beggar turned up at the end of convoy party demanding his medal and tee-shirt.

Apart from the fact that fate always intervenes when you least want it to, we have been have been fairly fortunate with all of our convoys.

The trucks always attracted thousands of admirers, they always personify professionalism and very rarely have they let us or their passengers down on the day of the convoy. Although one year not to long ago my own truck decided that it wanted a new battery on the morning of the convoy. Where did DAF aid decide to change the offending batteries? Only right at the front of the assembly area, and next to the visiting Lord Mayor!

I told people it was a publicity stunt, well I would, wouldn't I?

The 14th convoy to me is the one that we will have a very hard task to surpass as regards the standard of the trucks.

At the front of the convoy it is difficult to get a view of all the trucks; it is not usually possible for me to see a complete convoy until I receive my copy of the video. About the only place Mary and I get to see the convoy completely, is when we are going over the New Haven Bridge at Great Yarmouth.

I look back briefly and I see the convoy stretching way back along the A47.What a sight, 75 highly polished and presented trucks, my wishes and dreams had been met in full; and not one sodden Wendy House!

THE TRUCKERS.

The truckers, who I have mentioned at various times, are a very badly represented bunch of individuals. Nobody cares a jot about how they go about making a living. The only press and media coverage they seem to get is bad.

If a truck is involved in a road accident, the trucker is always to blame, if bad driving is the subject of a television debate, the poor old trucker will always come out worse than anybody else will.

On the day of the convoy, for just one day they are heroes. Why can't it last?

My tunnel vision like view on this one will never change. No one gives a toss about how anything gets from A to B in this island of ours. Not one haulage organization or publication ever tries to advertise the sterling and professional work performed by the British trucker. We the East Coast Truckers have done more in twenty years to promote the much-maligned industry, than the RHA and FTA have done in all of their existence. It is we who get the public to see that we are just normal people trying to earn a living. So if you do see our convoy, and you are a member of one of the afore-mentioned organizations, give your membership money to us, it will be better spent.

On our special day for the children, we are applauded, praised and liked; it feels great. We are not all monsters after all, the Convoy is a huge boost to our self-esteem, and perhaps Joe Public does love us after all. Yes, the East Coast Truckers Convoy gets us good publicity. It lets people see that we are not just a bunch of greasy fat uncouth road hogs. It lets them see the caring side to us. Do not get me wrong for one moment, I am not saying no other body of people could do the same as us or even better it. What I am trying to explain is that the convoy does more by the way of giving the haulage industry a better image, than all of the so-called professional representatives of the haulage industry.

We show the world that truckers are just the same as any other group of workers, we the East Coast Truckers have first hand experience of the type of people truckers really are. I have seen 15 stone truck drivers with hands like corn shovels reduced to quivering sobbing wrecks at the sight of the children they give up their hard-earned rest to take care of for just one day. These same men will give every last penny they have in the world, if it means one of our charges will have just one good day on this earth.

The truckers who have taken part in our convoys very often form lasting friendships with the families of the handicapped children and the feedback I receive is that their own lives and their family's lives are much enlightened because of the contact with such children and their families. I myself have known nothing but the problems and the stigma of disability because of my father's problems, my father was blown up during the Second World War; that is a story in itself, so I can only outline the exact event. His injuries were many but the worst of it was he lost both of his hands just above the wrists. So you can see I really do have first hand experience regards disability, it does give you a completely different perspective of life and how lucky most of us are. I again have three healthy sons and equally healthy grand children; makes you really grateful and humble when you are confronted, as we the East Coast Truckers regularly are, with the less fortunate.

Not all of the children invited are necessarily handicapped in any particular way. Some of them are what we consider to be underprivileged, as in the case of this particular story.

The child had been nominated by a caring relative, to take part in our convoy. On the morning of the convoy, it had been noted that the child was late; so our booking in system went into overdrive. Inquiries were made and a volunteer was found to go and collect the child in question. When our representative arrived at the address logged on to our fact sheet, a rather nasty fellow opened the door just wide enough to utter a few words I am unable to print here. Basically he said the child, a little girl, would not be coming on our convoy and could we go away! So our chap did just that.

Approximately 30 minutes later our chap arrived back at the same address, this time he had 3 other chaps with him; now I know some truckers look like they would have a hard time catching a cold, but wind them up, especially with something as emotional as our convoy and believe you me Iron Mike Tyson would think twice about biting lumps out of them! This time the door opened just far enough to get a fag paper through. That was far enough; a size 12 boot jammed it open far enough to get a tea tray sized hand in, the uncouth slob behind the door stood no chance at all. His last words to our departing party were, "Take the little cow then, and don't bother bringing her back".

Apparently, the poor little soul had not been out of her bedroom, apart from going to school, for very many weeks.

We were told by the relative who nominated the little girl that the girl has since been taken into care.

The weekend of the convoy means that the truckers who take part on our convoy, sacrifice a peaceful few days away from their truck and the white line. It means hours of cleaning and polishing. It means highs and lows on a very emotional day with the children. I have known truckers to be preparing their trucks for the convoy while waiting at the channel ports for a ferry back to England. One dedicated fellow arrived at the assembly point straight off the ferry; he had not seen his family for the best part of three weeks. I have witnessed truckers polishing their chassis and diesel tanks with an old toothbrush. I have seen them late on a Saturday night before the convoy polishing and preparing their trucks in the dark, with little more that a Tilley lamp to see by. I have seen them starting to prepare their trucks as many as four weeks before the convoy. Believe it or not, none of these actions is through vanity alone, and certainly not for the very mundane prize of a winner's cup. They do it to impress the thousands of people who line our route throughout the day of the convoy. They do it to make their child of the day feel even more special than they already are. Now try to tell me or anyone else for that matter, that these people deserve the appalling way they are perceived, persecuted, and treated. Yes, I may be biased, but just give up your time one bank holiday and see for yourself the kind of character we attract to the convoy. If we can convince just one of you that we are not at all like the type cast image often portrayed by the media, then my hours of hard work and theirs will have not been in vain.

THE CHILDREN.

Let it never be said that we have refused to accept a child onto our convoy because we could not be bothered to make allowances for their particular affliction or problem. Every single application will be dealt with on a one to one basis, if it is possible to get the child into the truck, that child will go on the convoy. If all else fails we have support vehicles and always have a large passenger coach. Nothing and I mean nothing will stand in our way of taking special needy children out for the day.

The only thing on this subject that will possibly be deemed negative is the fact that if a child comes on our convoy and upsets other children or acts in a violent way that even the more burly members of our team find difficult to deal with, then that child will be deemed unsuitable for future convoys. May I add that that situation happens very rarely?

I recall two of the children we had on our first ever convoy. One was called Mathew, I cannot remember the other lad's name, but Mathew was one of the most loving mentally handicapped children you would wish to meet. His one main failing was his ability to move like a gold medal sprinter, his energy was boundless, and while his eyes were open, he always moved like the proverbial whirlwind. He came with us on three convoys and we always had to put him with the same trucker. Ray Hodson, or 'Bannercheck' as most truckers know him, is one exceptional guy; he would insist year on year that Mathew would be with him. This worked out well really, because no one else would ever have Mathew: God bless you Ray.

The other child was not quite so endearing; he very nearly bit through the finger of one of our members wives. He, I am afraid only came with us the once.

We have even up until this present day, never formatted a type of child we would take on our convoy and we never will.

We have in place a very professionally minded team of people, their sole aim is to make sure that the children selected to join us are catered for the best way that suits their particular needs. If we decide that a child needs more specialized care than we can provide, then so be it. We will if need be hire the required expertise.

We always have on hand truckers who can lift and support the most difficult case. If you have never tried to support or lift a child of any size who is paralyzed from the neck down, you will have a difficult time visualizing the problem; one of our helpers from a well-known charity said it was easier to lift spaghetti of a plate with a pair of chopsticks while blindfolded. I think I understand what he was trying to say.

At the time of writing over 1800 children have benefited from the Children's Convoy. All of them are treated like royalty, but it is very difficult after all this time to remember but a few of them but one little girl comes readily to mind. She is now well into her twenties.

Heidi Everitt first came on one of our early convoys. She was obviously extremely physically and mentally handicapped, nevertheless an inspiration. A few years after she came on her first convoy she was the subject of a BBC television documentary. The documentary was produced to publicize the advent of the very high compensation claims now being awarded to victims of accidents.

Heidi's own personal case was quite unique in so much that her lawyers had sued her very own mother. Her mother, Pam, was driving Heidi in her car, when she hit a puddle at an awkward spot on a tree-lined road. The car went out of control. Heidi was so severely injured that she was not expected to live. She did however survive but with a severely handicapped body; I am not qualified to say what the injuries were and it is not relevant to the story in general. All I can say is that she was awarded a British record payout against her own mother. As part of the documentary, the film crew followed Heidi on her trip with us on our convoy.

Heidi is doing great, and although she no longer comes on the convoy she can be seen with her mother waving crazily as the convoy goes past. We know that she will be in the same place every year. God bless you Heidi.

We, the truckers, have all bonded with the children in our care for the day and it is true to say we thoroughly spoil them. Nothing is ever too much trouble or a problem. If you have never had any kind of contact with handicapped people at all, especially children, your lives will always be less enhanced and much poorer.

They will give you a sense of purpose; they will give you an outlook on life deeper and more fulfilling than any thing else.

Moreover, you appreciate, if only for a short time how lucky you and your able-bodied children are.

Every year we are fortunate enough to be able to introduce new truckers to the convoy. We are always discreetly asked by new drivers and their wives the same question. "Please can you give me a child that is not to badly handicapped?" "Why?" I ask. They never can really find a proper reason, but I suspect some people find it hard to handle the situation that we throw them into. Mary and I do not have a problem with that; neither do most of our hard-core members. Subsequently we will never put a severely handicapped child with any one other than our most experienced people. One tip we always give strangers to our convoy is to treat the children like royalty because they are with us, and not because they seem different from able-bodied or more fortunate children. They may have been given a very bad deal on this earth but they are still members of the human race. I also tell them that the difference between all of us is a very fine line.

One spiky little chap brought all of my theories home many convoys ago. He was wheel chair bound; he would never have a life like most of us. His future was to be much the same every day until he died. He was being pushed around Pleasurewood Hills by friends of his own age group; they were lads from the school he attended. He was the life and soul of any gathering, constantly cracking jokes and laughing with any body he came into contact with. I will remember one of the jokes he told me to my last day on this earth.

"Hey Glenn", he shouted, "What is the hardest thing about eating vegetables?" "Go on hit me with it then". I replied. "The bloody wheelchair", he chirped. From that day on, I learned a very valuable lesson: laugh with them and not at them. Never be afraid of disability or handicapped persons.

There is also a well-known cliché that says good people will receive their reward in heaven. Why wait? Work with the handicapped and get your rewards now; we do.

THE SAINTS

Apart from the afore-mentioned Truckers, their Trucks and the Children there is one other element that makes our convoy work. It is the 'Saints' and dozens of unnamed helpers. Some are our own hard working members; others are ordinary people who just want to help. They are all invaluable and in most cases modest and quite humble about the significant role that they play. We need them as much as the air we breathe.

Over the course of the last twenty convoys, we have had many a funny situation and only a few sad ones. We have been helped by a succession of various people. It would need a very thick book and a very good memory to enlighten you about all of them.
So all I can do is take out the best bits and the bits I would consider to be of interest to you as the patient reader.
In the process of this story, I will touch upon very many occurrences that link or directly revolve around our convoy. It is by far the most important achievement of the East Coast Truckers Club. Many clubs would literally commit murder just to have something only half as successful as our convoy. This would be a good point in our story to explain that although Mary and I ran the first convoys in their entirety, all be it on a budget, it would be quite impossible for us to do the same now.

If you witness the convoys now you would hardly recognize them from their earliest forms. As with all things, you get either bigger or better, or you die. We now have our convoy team, a well versed, well educated, well informed, and totally committed to the smooth running of the only event of its kind anywhere in the world (to the best of our knowledge). This team functions as one body when need be and as individuals when it matters, we do not have vast plutocratic policies to stifle or hinder. They all know what is to be done, and apply effort accordingly.

That aside, there exists another small army of people; these are our generous fundraisers, scroungers and hard working helpers, found at all of the many events we involve ourselves with year in and year out. These kind souls are not members; they do not want to be members and many of them because of the constitution of the club can never be members. Although thanks to the introduction of Friends of the ECT that situation has now been rectified. They are the only reason we are able to go from strength to strength every year, they make our lives so much easier. Who are they? Where do they come from and why do they work so tirelessly with little recognition and no reward?

The first answer is easy; they are all saints; secondly, the East Coast Truckers have always had the ability to bring out the very best in the most humble of people. Finding a third reason will be a little harder to define. If you were to ask any of the unsung heroes that very same question, they could never find an answer.

I do, however, have a very good and well-substantiated answer.

They do what they do because they derive pleasure from helping others. Perverse it may be to people who would rather watch than do. I see the joy of life come into their faces when they are with us or helping us. I see the energy bounding from them. Coupled with the enthusiasm, you would not believe unless you were to see with your own eyes, that some of these people are well into their retirement years. Yes, we also have younger helpers; they are the generation that most of the older ones among us would rather criticize, than praise.

I think that we have a knack of bringing out the saint in people young or old and long may we continue to do so.

The very first person who comes to mind here is someone very special and dear to me. She is Mrs. Doreen Johnson, my mother. I know, call me sycophantic, bring nepotism into the equation Nevertheless, she is one of the saints and to give you a rough idea that her efforts are doubly valued, I will have to give you a very brief account of her life to date. She was born more than 80 years ago, to a mother and father she would never get to know. She still lives but a short bus ride from the house where she spent her childhood. Many people of my mother's generation do. She has never had a passport and I do not think she ever will. My mother was brought up by her grandmother. Every day after school, she would collect and deliver other peoples laundry. Her grandmother took in other peoples washing to supplement a very meagre income.

That was about the extent of her childhood; no fancy trips to theme parks or foreign school trips that my Grandchildren and no doubt all of our children take for granted. She fell in love and married my father sixty years ago. Nothing much unusual about that you may say, but there is much more to all of this than you may imagine.

My father is a one hundred percent disabled war pensioner; as I mentioned earlier he lost both of his hands just above the wrists in the very last weeks of world war two. My mother has devoted her entire life to caring for his every need for all those sixty years. She has been the subject of his tantrums and some times justifiable violent mood swings. She has nursed him when he has been sick and there has never been, in all those years, even one day when she has not been there for him. Not only that, she brought up two children, my brother Carl and me. Although we were brought up in abject poverty, we never went hungry and we never went without basic items of clothing; but we never really knew any different, and we were loved and brought up with dignity and righteousness.

In spite of all her troubles and sacrifice, I only have to ask my mother a favour regards our children's charity or Convoy and it is as good as done. She now divides her time, even at her great age in life between raising funds for our charity, the Cobholm Community Centre, my father and anybody else with half a sob story.

We all love our mums; even long after they have left us. I too, love my mum dearly. Not only that the East Coast Truckers love my mum equally as I do. Thanks mum.

The day after one of our convoys some years ago, I received a phone call from a lady calling herself Betty from Halvergate.

To this day, I still know her as BETTY FROM HALVERGATE as do all of the older members of the club. But for the purposes of this story her name is Betty Tortice. Betty is yet another example of extreme human kindness.

The convoy had been running to Pleasurewood Hills for several years, when we decided to take the children to somewhere quite different. Pettit's at Reedham was a very low-key zoo come nature park. On our route through to Pettit's we travelled passed a small community known to us as Halvergate. The local people all came out to wish us well, both on our journey in and out of the park. One of those local people was Betty. Betty approached me while we were at Pettit's and stated, "We as the community of Halvergate would like to raise money for you and the children, may we have your permission?" was her very polite request. And so it was. Betty along with her family and friends sprang into action. They raised money in so many ways it is hard to keep up with them, even to this day. We still of course attend the Halvergate Fete and all thoroughly enjoy our day with Betty and her friends, and of course her lovely cakes.

We do not go to Pettit's any more but on our way through to Great Yarmouth the convoy passes the turn off to the village of Halvergate on the A47, every year. Without fail, many of the people who

66

helped us can be seen along with their families, waving and cheering as we go by. Thank you Betty and the good people of Halvergate.

While I am on the subject of Pettit's, I have a very amusing story to tell. I was having a well-earned cup of tea in Pettit's tearoom, when one of the Pettit's managers came looking for me. "I have two people from the nearby village to see you Mr. Johnson", she said. My first thought was the negative one of here comes a compliant; not so. The two people announced themselves as members of the village business community, and they would like us very much to take our convoy through the village of Reedham on our way to Great Yarmouth. What a lovely request; normally people cannot see the back of us quicker enough.

I said yes we would, subject to travelling the route and checking for any hazards we may encounter. So I, Bernie, (Heidi's Dad) and Sergeant Dick Howard set off around the proposed route.
The only problem we could find was some of the trees were to low, so a team was sent out armed with a handsaw and aboard our open top double-decker bus, to cut back any offending branches. (Most modern super trucks are the best part of 13 feet high.) At 4oclock, we set off by special request to travel along the waterfront of Reedham and the village. That is by far the smallest place we have ever taken the convoy. Tight is an understatement, a fag paper would not have much room to breathe between the trucks and the walls of the houses. As we made our very slow journey through the village, generous visitors and villagers were giving us money, sweets, chocolate and ice creams. A warm welcome we will all remember for years to come. We do have the knack bring out the very best in people.

One last occurrence about Reedham; as we were making our way through the village, I spied two very exited people on a very smart looking cruiser; they were jumping up and down, waving and shouting frantically to all the trucks and truckers. There was our very good friend, WALLY WEBB along with the delectable and quite delicious SHERI.

It would be fair to say that Wally would, over the coming years, have a more profound effect on the convoy than any other member of the media would. His name has cropped up on more than one occasion in this story and I suppose he was destined to help our cause. His involvement really took flight after Convoy eleven.

The chairman of the East Coast Truckers that year was Gerry King. He received a telephone call from his father-in-law the morning after one of our convoys. Radio Norfolk's Wally Webb had been talking about the previous day's convoy on his Monday morning radio programme and was requesting information from his listeners about what the convoy was all about. Our Gerry immediately rang Wally and in a very articulate way explained live on air the theme and intentions of the East Coast Truckers Convoy.

Ultimately, Gerry and I were invited into the studio for several Sunday mornings to chat with Wally about the club and the convoy.

To blow our own trumpets, we were so good at this radio malarkey; we were starting to get fan mail! Is that why you stopped having us on your programme Wally?

No, all joking aside Wally has demonstrated what the power of the media can do; since those very early interviews on his programme we have reached a much larger proportion of the local community.

It was the start of the convoy getting real recognition, although it is fair to say that we have now gained access to other and possibly greater forms of media; Wally will always be our number one broadcaster, and since the founding of our Charity, he is now a valued and much loved patron. He has also over the years, not been just a very good friend to The East Coast Truckers, but to Mary and myself my children. We love you WALLY, you keep doing us proud.

It was while on one of Wally's radio programme that I announced that we were to auction a very special place on the convoy. I have, apart from only one year, been the lead truck and convoy leader. I have become a little bit blasé after so many convoys, as to the spectacle we in the lead truck are witness to every year. Nevertheless, I thought it would be a very good way of raising money for Wally's very own charity as a way of thanking him for his support. It was my intention to invite one of Wally's listeners to experience the delights of riding in the lead truck for the whole day.

We ran the same scheme for 5 years. The very first time we ran the auction it was won by a very generous lady for her husband's birthday. Hilda and Ron had by chance seen the convoy make its way though the village of Reedham, some years earlier. Ron had expressed his wish to be part of the convoy; she put in a fantastic bid of over £400. She begged us not to tell Ron how much she paid. We got to know Ron quite well over the next few years. Hilda need not have worried about Ron's reaction to the large sum of money she had donated. Ron himself donated even more 2 years later so that Hilda could experience the same delights that he had enjoyed on our convoy. Ron very sadly died a few years ago, albeit much richer and wiser for knowing us. I just know that every year we run our convoy that 'the Rons' of this world are still with us. Every year we can still see Hilda waving as we go by. Good bless and keep you Ron.

Enter one other very charitable, and I must say very prominent, person; Elsie Bertram MBE. Elsie was a regular listener to Wally's radio programme and also a personal friend of his. At one of our visits to Wally's house, we met the very energetic and amiable Elsie. Elsie along with her late husband formed the Bertram book empire. Although now retired from the business, she still devotes all her time to fundraising for her favourite Diabetes Charity. She expressed her desire, even at her great age to ride in the lead truck and thrust a check for £500 into my hand. So it was, she had her day in the lead truck and even with all the great things she has done and all of the very important people she has met and known, she said that she will never forget the experience and excitement to her dying day. We have, since our first encounter with Elsie, received more help and money than she would ever admit to. Obviously, her obligations are to her own charity but we know we only have to call her and help would be at hand.

I must tell you a very amusing but ironic story all about Elsie, it goes as thus. I can candidly recall the rather unpleasant but sometimes expected compliant in the Eastern Daily Press the local paper, after one of our convoys. The compliant read:
"Who do these nasty smelly truck drivers think they are? My Sunday morning was totally ruined when well before midday I was woken from my slumber by the most awful racket you could ever imagine. The abominable noise went on for ages. Have not these lay-abouts anything else to do with their Sundays? I am in a good mind to report this load of thugs to the police.'"

Well, Elsie read the letter in her paper. If you know her, you will know that there is not a great deal of muscle and brawn on her not too young body. If she could have gotten to our good friend she would have been hard pressed not to do him physical harm. She immediately phoned the editor of the local paper. After she had severely bent his ear, she went to work on a letter to the same paper and many other papers. The scathing attack on our now rather nervous friend, continued for very many paragraphs. It also sparked a rash of other letters in our support. Our poor old 'Mr.Ihavenothingelsetodo' must have been wondering what he could do to get the heat off! He did, in the end, write again to the paper explaining that he knew nothing about what we were doing and that he was sorry to cause offence.

(Sadly the loveable Elsie died, age 89, in 2002.)

While we are talking about people who have made a very substantial contribution to all things that the East Coast Truckers have attempted or been involved with, it would be very unfair not to mention another man, Rod Green. Although it was very late in the history of the convoy when I happened upon this man, like most things that have come about, it seemed that he was tailor made if not even chosen for us by a much higher authority.

At the end of all our convoys, we have a winding down party or gathering. At this little soiree, we hand out awards to all the participating truckers. We thank a lot of people and announce the winners of the much-coveted Best Kept Truck competition.

It was at one of these after convoy events, that I received a message from one of the committee. He said, "There is a chap about here somewhere that wants to speak to you".

He continued, the best way he could over all the noisy hubble, "I think he said his name was Big Rod".

After ploughing my way through the milling crowds of the after convoy throng, I came across an absolutely enormous man sitting quite alone waiting for me to appear. The very first thing he said to me, even before any niceties was, "Are you a registered charity?" My reply was a very definite "No". His next word was "Why?"

The thought had crossed my mind on numerous occasions but had never manifested itself as a possibility or seemed a feasible idea. He continued, "Get yourselves charity status and I can help you in ways you never even dreamed of". "By the way my name is Rod, people know me as Big Rod". I thought to myself, "I wonder why?"

Rod is the kind of man who has little time for trivia, he sees a target and will not except a negative response. If he wants the answer to be yes, you can bet your cotton socks the answer will be yes. He most definitely could sell a long nose to Pinocchio. I remember him telling me that while waiting for one of our convoys to return from Great Yarmouth, he and his long-suffering wife Lynn retrieved two bottles of wine complete with glasses from the boot of their car and promptly started to sell it to other waiting members of the public. All proceeds went to the East Coast Truckers. That is our Big Rod.

Rod was born, just north of London at a place called Epping. That's where they eat cake with forks! He left school to take up an apprentice as a wood machinist; this proved detrimental to Rod's health so he started to chauffeur the rich and famous around the big smoke. After a couple of stressful redundancies he decided to go it alone. Gladly he has made it a total success and is still in business right up to this present day. He met and married the delectable Lynn and between them they have Mark a grown up son.

Rod is a keen fisherman and, so in the little leisure time he has, Heacham seemed an ideal place to be to indulge pastime; Heacham being next to the sea. Wherever he finds time to systematically drown worms I will never know; the man is a nuclear dynamo.

Lynn told me of his thirst for charity and there are not enough pages available in this story to fit in all of his achievements and conquests.

One of his earliest fund raising gambits was for the Guide Dogs for the Blind Association. He and Lynn organized a sponsored walk taking in all eleven London Bridges. They raised over £4000. He was hooked. The scouts were another group that benefited from the energy and enthusiasm of our Rod. If that were not enough, because of his connections with the sea he has a fond affection for helping the RNLI.

After falling in love with the North Norfolk coastline, he and Lynn bought a small cottage in the village. You might have guessed it was not long before our Rod was heavily into helping the local community anyway he could.

After Rod and Lynn, and not forgetting Mark, became involved with the club they immediately started to donate all of the money they raised on their market-type stall to the children's convoy. They sold CDs, Books, Cassettes and anything else they could requisition from companies who would lose the will to live rather than say no to Big Rod. Rod is constantly looking for ways to raise even more money. I could not keep up with the man; and I just get carried along by his boundless energy. At the grand age of 55 he thought it would be a good idea to apply to run the London Marathon, for not just us, but also a couple of other deserving causes. Now I do not want to sound critical here but Rod is not exactly what you would recognize as the shape or size made for long distance running, in fact I would describe him as having the aerodynamic qualities of a breezeblock. Did he do it? If I have explained his qualities accurately, you will know the answer.

He turned up at a meeting and quite casually thrust a cheque for the best part of £5000 in my hand. Beat that!

It is often said by way of a compliment that some people wear their hearts on their sleeves, that being the case Rods heart is a three-piece suit.

Did we become a charity? That is another chapter.

Rod, although no longer part of the Charity, his valuable input will always be valued and remembered. I have mentioned earlier some people draw strength from helping others less fortunate, Rod proves my point quite emphatically. I will always be grateful to Rod for his guidance his vision and his knowledge. Our charity would never have been instigated if it were not for him. It was great shame we could not take our alliance any further. He was a truly great man and an inspiration. He left us with a better idea of how we should conduct ourselves at committee level. The reason he left us partly falls at my door. Let me explain. I protected the Children's Convoy with as much vigour as I protected my own children. Rod's energy and enthusiasm was a great asset to us and other organizations but he tried to marginalize our convoy. He loved the convoy without question, but his wish to divert attention away from the convoy and onto his own projects was not going to wash with me at all. We had more than one big disagreement about that matter as well as various niggling things. I could have lived with that, but the biggest threat came from the gapping crack that was appearing between The Club and the newly formed Charity. The wellbeing of the convoy was being threatened by the very body we had set up to help fund and promote it. We were in serious trouble; it was at this time I took legal action to protect my life's work. The only way we could salvage the situation was to go back to just one committee. The Club had set a precedent over the years by only allowing HGV licence holders to be eligible for the executive committee positions. The abolition of the second committee meant that Rod, not being a licence holder was not going to be re-elected. As a mark of respect, he was offered the role as Vice-President. A role he never took up and sadly, we lost touch with him in 2003.

MONEY, MONEY, MONEY.

The actual cost of our Children's Convoy is quite impossible to calculate. These days it seems as if everything from the cost of a toothbrush to having a baby has to have a price and a balance sheet that we can all see

72

and understand. That being the case I can give a rough calculation at today's prices. You will appreciate that the time and love given by all of us who donate their free time and energy is near on impossible to put down as pounds and pence! We always field a minimum of 75 trucks; each of these trucks cost their respective owners between £65,000 and £100,000 to purchase. The road fund licence and insurance can add about another £9,000 per annum. On the day of the convoy, each truck will consume about 25 gallons of fuel at a cost of about £100.00.

Then there is the cost of tee-shirts, baseball caps, food, and entrance fees to whichever venue we are taking the children to. Therefore, you can see that the cost is enormous; we roughly calculate the day to cost some where in the region of £14,000. Add to that the time and good will of all the people involved and you can see that special days do not come cheap.

We do not consider, however, any of the cost at all. Whatever the cost is, it is repaid with the joy and satisfaction we get from helping others. Nevertheless, we have to fund the day somehow. We always have an abundance of people who are willing to help us in our quest for money. These kind souls are indispensable.

One of our first major fund raisers was the Watton Show. Watton is situated between Norwich and the Fens. If you were to sneeze on you way along the A1075 you would miss it, but it is a well-organized show with a long history. We take our own trucks along, for people to see and photograph, with loved ones in the cabs. We also take along three trucks loaned to us by the Norwich Training Service (NTS) for members of the public to drive. The public are given guidance and help by our most experienced club members, and they drive on the now disused runway of the airfield that the show takes place on.

The lady members of the club run various stalls and we also take the younger children around the circuit in some of the trucks. We are on hand all day to answer questions about the job we do and of course about the trucks themselves.

The Watton Show is the start to our fund raising year, so I suppose the Police Gala Day held at the Royal Norfolk Show Ground, Norwich would be, in all probability, our last fund raising event of the year: with whatever may come our way anywhere in between these two events. We are always looking for new ways to raise money.

The Police Gala Day used to be the weekend before our convoy so it is a good chance to get the trucks all polished up in readiness for our

73

own big show. The Police have organized this event with the help of Radio Norfolk, the local BBC radio station. A vintage and classic car rally also takes place there and this in itself attracts some 500 entries every year. In the main show ring there is a full day's entertainment. The entertainment ranges from stunt men to dog agility displays.

The Norfolk Show ground is a vast area and to fill it takes very many stands, displays and stalls to make it look anywhere near full. Every year the police improve on all previous years and we, the truckers follow their example. This is the one fundraising event totally supported by all our members. Good job too because we always have at least four or five different things for the paying public to do.

We have the training school trucks for people to drive around a well-supervised route. We take children for rides in our members road trucks; we have various competitions running all day, one of which is a competition where people are invited to get a tennis ball into a beer glass. That does not sound too difficult, does it? Except they have to do it with a full sized JCB digger! It is on this day that we take a truck and a few of the convoy organizers over to the Radio Norfolk outside broadcast stand. There, the lovely Sheri Webb will be waiting for us. She will give us the low-down as to when Wally will be fitting us into his rather hectic schedule.

Radio Norfolk broadcasts for the entire day and it is a very good opportunity to give our forthcoming convoy a plug.

Now I know that this is not the first time I have mentioned Wally and now would be as good a time as any to dedicate a paragraph or two to him and obviously Sheri.

You will remember our first ever introduction to Wally at our FUN DAYS, many years previously and subsequently he has crossed our paths many times before. I will not drum on about all the help and inspiration he has given us over the years, or all the plugs he has given us about a multitude of things. What I will do is give you a little bit of insight into the man himself.

Wally was born, as he would say, when he was very young. To be precise he was born in 1949, and his early years were spent in his home town of Eccles. He left school to start a right old assortment of jobs, from hairdressing to bus driving. After he had attempted every job in and around the Manchester area, he thought it would be a good career move to join the Royal Air Force. They must have literally hundreds of different jobs for our Wally. He nevertheless ended up as a statistician. The RAF stationed Wally at Coltishal, near Norwich; it was while he was serving at Coltishal, that he first got the bug for being a Disc Jockey. He set up a mobile disco called SOLARSCOPE and traipsed it all over the surrounding area. He then secured himself a lucrative job as a resident DJ at the then famous Scamps Night Club in Norwich.

Hospital Radio was probably his first crack at broadcasting. At least your audience could not escape, eh Wally! Radio Norfolk had just been commissioned by the BBC and Wally applied for a job. He is, to this day the longest serving member of the broadcast team and the only survivor of the original starting line-up. You cannot say he is not a sticker.

It was at one of Radio Norfolk's outside broadcasts that he met and fell in love with Sheri. Sheri is a real Norfolk gal. Although she has no local accent, she comes from real Norfolk farming stock.

Born on a farm at Lenwade and educated at Wymondham, her first job on leaving school was as a clerical assistant at the City Hall.

Fate was set when she went to work for the beeb. They married a year after meeting and have been blissfully happy ever since.

Wally and Sheri are now considered as two of the dearest friends Mary and I have. Reward in itself, for merely helping to run the most successful trucking club in the whole of the UK.

Wally is another one of the people, we just know, will be there as long as there is an East Coast Truckers Convoy. Take a bow from us Wally. Wally is now a patron of the Charity.

Back at the Police Gala Day, Wally eventually gets to our neatly parked truck near to the BBC outside broadcast stand. Wally always climbs up into the cab of the truck we have taken around for him, and he describes to his listeners, with some detail the interior of the truck. It is old hat to us but I guess many people must be interested in the trucks. We know from our own feedback that the trucks always attract a large amount of attention wherever we take them. It is at these little live interviews with Wally that we let people know our timetable for the following week. We say our goodbyes to Wally and his listeners with the usual blast of a 130-decibel air horn. He just loves that.

It was at one of the Police Gala days that I remember with a certain amount of fear, being secretly nominated to be the passenger in a stunt car. You may remember a television advertisement some years ago, depicting a car that hops up on to its side and manoeuvres between a very narrow doorway. The same car then does a very fast handbrake turn and parks perfectly between two cars, with but a few inches to spare. Well the same chap who performed the stunt for the advertisement took a show on the road, travelling the country and visiting various outdoor events. The police gala day was one such event. He always asked for an able-bodied volunteer to be his victim and passenger, I was the man thanks to my wonderful friends and colleagues who nominated me for the task. Now I am a fairly tolerant passenger. If you have ever driven with my eldest son you will know what I mean but this bloke was a pawn short of a chess set. My stomach was doing somersaults quicker than the rest of my body. Boy was I glad when the demonstration was over!

Although it was an experience not everybody is privileged to endure, I don't think I want to be a stunt man's stooge ever again.

The Police Gala day is always looked upon by the club as a very good source for raising large amounts of money and every year we succeed in breaking all our records. This is mainly due to the hard work of just about all of our members. I have mentioned the fact many times, but the main ingredient for this success is the fact that we have loads of fun while we are working. I have a theory that if you raise a million pounds and have no fun the day is a failure but if you raise one pound and everyone has a great time the day is total success.

CONVOY DAY.

The August Bank Holiday Sunday, is without question the most important day of the year, not just for me but the East Coast Truckers and all of its members and of course of our army of helpers.

All of our plans and fund raising culminates to this one-day. We live and breathe as a club and charity just for this day. It would be fair to say that the Convoy has held the club together through some very precarious times, so I think we owe as much to the convoy as it owes to us.

My own day of the convoy starts around about 5.00am. If I have not had enough time the previous day to prepare and polish my own truck to the standards required, I have to get up even earlier to complete that very important task. My first job is to turn on the television and any other media source I can find, to ascertain what we can expect as regards the weather. Now everybody who organizes outdoor events in Great Britain worries constantly about the weather. This is for fairly obvious reasons. Punters normally stay indoors when the weather is inclement. Who can blame them?

76

My worries are compounded by one other fact that most people are totally unaware of.

The 75 to 80 trucks we run on the convoy are designed for the specific task of hauling extremely heavy loads coupled up to a 13 metre trailer. When you take the tractive unit away from the trailer, you are operating the truck in an alien environment. It loses a lot of its traction; the brakes lose some of their responsiveness and the trucks can become quite unstable. With all of this in mind you will have some idea that rain on convoy day is my biggest fear, from the time I get up on that Sunday morning until the time I get the trucks safely back with their precious cargos to Norwich; I am constantly monitoring the weather.

If that were not enough I also have the worry of eight police motorcyclists; again not very good machines when the roads are sopping wet.

I thank God for the fact that not more than three of our convoys have had significantly enough rain to spoil our day, and only one where the weather was bad for the best part of the day.

At about 6.30am I drag my poor family out to the truck. We load up all the necessary items we will need for the day. Even though my role as convoy leader and overall controller takes precedence, Mary and I still have to take care of a guest child for the day.

It would be fair to say Mary and my three boys have always done me proud here. They know, full well, I will be anywhere but helping them with our charge for the day; they always take care of that side of things without any complaints.

The truck loaded up, we make our way down to our starting point. From 2004, the assembly point became County Hall. Prior to that, it was the Norwich Livestock Market where the B&Q superstore now stands. The livestock market was our third starting point over the years, the first being Repton House, the second was the Castle Plain car park.

As I pull onto the assembly point, a highly organized team will already be hard at work. All the truck places would have been marked out with each having a number. The trucks will be guided to a reception area where the driver will receive his instructions for the day, a timetable, a tee-shirt for himself and one for his charge for the day, a sun strip for the windscreen of the truck and any other bits and pieces that may be being issued for that day.

The truck is then be escorted to its designated parking slot.

By 8.00am 75% of the donated trucks will be in place, the whole place will be bedlam. All the organizers will have a particular task and they do it well every year but nothing ever runs true to plan, so I have to be on hand every single minute.

It is nothing for at least three people to be looking for me at the same time, it may look like uncontrolled mayhem to outsiders but we do know what we are doing.

At 9.15am sharp a drivers briefing is called. This is for drivers only, for obvious reasons. It will be difficult enough for me to keep the convoy safe without the left hand knowing what the right one is doing.

I must digress here for a moment to tell you of a story you just could not make up, this really did happen!

The Saturday evening before the convoy I received a phone call from a member who was supposed to be coming on our convoy the next day, "I cannot come tomorrow" he said, "Why", I asked thinking something dreadful had happened. "My wife says I am not to come", he said. "Pardon", I said, "Why won't she let you come? You know if you have pledged a truck you cause all kinds of problems if you fail to turn up", I said. "Here you better talk to her", he said. "I am angry about the letter you sent to all the members", she said. All candidates for the convoy receive in the post a small but very important set of dos and don'ts for the day. In this letter, we also tell everybody about the timetable and any other points we see as being necessary. I also mention that the drivers briefing will be held at a certain time and that all drivers, and only drivers, are to attend. The women had taken great exception that she, not being a driver, was excluded from the drivers briefing. Now for one thing we hold the briefing in a very small annex and the only people required to attend a drivers briefing are drivers. Every person I have come across in all the years we have been running the convoy, have had no problem at all in grasping this very simple fact.

The telephone conversation went seriously down hill after she had called me a jumped up little 'jobs worth', in fact I found myself getting dragged into a slanging match. I do not need this the night before convoy day. Needless to say these people will never be invited on to our convoy ever again.

Back to our briefing:

The briefing is carried out with serious aims but is usually conducted with much banter. Once we have got all the usual jokes out of the way about

78

A collection of photographs of Trucks on the East Coast Truckers'
Children's Convoys. (From Betty Tortice)

85

Betty Tortice

86

my lack of height; mocked each other on any of a dozen subjects we get down to the serious business of conducting the convoy in a thoroughly safe and professional manner.

In recent years, one of our motorcycle team will attend the briefing and interject any points he sees as being important to the safe running of the convoy.

I will announce the CB frequency we will be using for the day with the usual request to keep all information given on this channel to be brief and to the point. At every briefing, I make a well-exaggerated point about the sensible use of air horns. The air horns on modern trucks are noisy to say the least; the children, truckers and most of the people watching the convoy just love to hear them, but anything up to 150 decibels can be a bit daunting for those people and animals that can be frightened by such loud blasts of noise. For that reason, we have a code that we expect all truckers participating on the convoy to adhere to. Most of the truckers comply with the simple request when the order is given to cease use of the air horns. It is a pity though that the 'numpties' who control the horse drawn carriages on Great Yarmouth's Golden Mile do not have the same discipline and common sense. Every year we make a request to the carriage operators, to keep their horses a few yards off the sea front for the half an hour that we are passing. Yes, I know that they have a right to earn a living, but they all know we are coming, and they know that their horses become stressed with so much noise. Do they help the horses, or us? No.

I will also notify the drivers of any unusual occurrences they may have to be ready for and emphasize the fact we must, as professional drivers, concentrate at all times. This point I repeat over, and over again, and again, for the simple reason that it is very easy for drivers to be carried away with all that is happening around them and forget the buck stops with them when it all goes wrong.

We have had very few catastrophes and we would rather have not had even them.

One happened as we were coming out of Pleasurewood Hills one year. We were starting to regroup when one of our convoy members saw a gap developing. He quite rightly saw the need to close the gap, accelerated a little too hard just as the truck in front was slowing down It was the first day on the road for our member's £90,000 truck. A bad set of circumstances and bad luck saw thousands of pounds worth of damage done in less time than it takes to utter obscenities. Fortunately only pride was hurt, although poor old Bart from Mildenhall nearly soiled his trousers when Big Mark Fuller caught up with him at the after convoy party. Now if you know Big Mark you will know that he has hands like corn shovels and Bart is a bit petite to say the least. Even though it was not Bart's fault, he was mighty relieved when Mark admitted that he had been a bit careless. "Only metal and plastic", said Mark, through clenched teeth

With all of this in mind you can now see my need for drumming on about concentration. I also explain the need for keeping the convoy as closely grouped as it is safe to do. We have limited resources as far as the police motorcyclists are concerned and the last thing we need is other road users jumping into any gap they see; and believe you me they will. Any offending car drivers are hooked out of the convoy the moment they are seen, but it is our aim not to give them the opportunity to get in, in the first place.

I thank all the drivers for preparing their trucks to the very high standards we have come to expect. I also announce that there will be the usual best kept or prepared truck competition, which at some stage will mean one of the judges looking at their particular truck. I also explain that this is a very tongue in cheek competition and they must not take it too seriously. We used to have one bunch of drivers come from a particular local firm that took it all too seriously and if they did not get on to the winners' sheet they got a little agitated. Shame they could not see the bigger picture because now we do not see anyone from this particular firm at all.

With all the details out of the way, I wish them all well and close the meeting.

Sometime between 9:00am and 9:15am, the Lord Mayor of the City of Norwich arrives with his or her consort. Mary and one of our other organizers will be on hand to meet them the minute that they arrive at the assembly point. They are shown around the now completely assembled convoy, they meet the children and the truckers and their families. I have been told, on more than one occasion, that this is one of the highlights in their busy year, for many of the serving Mayors we have invited along for the convoy.

Since the demise of the livestock market, our new location is the Norfolk County Hall, and we now have what I would call dignitary overload, we are now waved off by not only the lord Mayor of Norwich but also the Norfolk County Council and no less than the Lord Lieutenant of Norfolk, who is the queens representative. Beat that!

At 9:30am our police motorcycle team arrives. Their arrival always attracts much attention, not just because people know that we are close to departing but also because the police are held with such high regard by all of the people who have attended our convoys before. Everybody knows, full well, the police motorcyclists are utterly indispensable. We are very fortunate in Norfolk to have a very good and understanding Police force, especially the traffic department.

I mentioned in detail earlier about our relationship with Dick Howard, our first ever police officer. I am very glad to say that the sound and solid relationship has continued throughout all the years. After Dick came Sgt John Himpleman and now we have Wes and Andy, by the time I finish this account we may have some one else but they will all have the same dedication to our cause. How humbling is that?

We also have the support of the whole of Norfolk Constabulary network; they assist in every way possible, something that we do not take lightly or for granted.

I being the representative of the East Coast Truckers and the Convoy Director, whom the buck stops with, regard the operating of the convoy the single most important thing that I do. I abide by whatever wishes the police have and whatever rules or requests that they may deem necessary. Although it is fair to say in keeping with the theme of the convoy, even the police keep the rules and regulations to a minimum.

It is always a struggle for me to get to the police motorcyclists. Hundreds of well-wishers and people wishing them a safe journey always surround them. After greeting them all in turn, my next task is talking to the police motorcyclist who will ride point, i.e. the poor soul who will have to dribble along at a snails pace in front of the lead truck.

We ascertain if we are likely to have any problems on route. He takes a tally of the exact number of trucks; and, of course, I ask about the weather. The police had a direct line to the weather station at RAF Coltishal very handy! *Well they did when Coltishall was still there!*

At about 9.50am I start making my final rounds of the assembled trucks, making last minute checks that all lights are on and everybody is loaded up and ready for the off. As I appear the crescendo of noise is absolutely deafening. The tension is now starting to build.

The Lord Mayor of Norwich will be on the observation platform of the United Road Transport Union's display trailer.

89

He, or She, will have been presented with a very large bouquet, and a few other pieces of memorabilia; and all the usual press photographs will have been taken.

The local television station will have sent along a film crew and a reporter. They would have set themselves up at a predetermined place of advantage.

I climb into the cab of the lead truck, my engine would have been started earlier by one of my helpers or one of my sons, avoiding the obvious need for me to warm up before the off. My heart at this stage, even after all these years, is still pumping like a road drill. The police are given the nod by me to say that we are all loaded up and ready go. I slip my truck into the lowest gear possible to start the slow drive by passing the waiting Lord Mayor. The noise behind me now is indescribable.

As I approach the exit, I can already see that hundreds of well-wishers are waiting for us. This is when it hits me; we really do matter to very many people; the proof is here for all to see; the months of hard work have now been justified. Even before I have cleared the exit, Sheri Webb will be on the mobile, "I have Wally coming to you after this record are you ready Glenn?" I hear the remnants of a song playing down the phone, then Wally explaining to his listeners that the East Coast Truckers Children's Convoy is on its way. "I have on the line the President of the East Coast Truckers and convoy leader, Mr. Glenn Johnson, how's it going Glenn?"

I then give a brief but informative account of how things are shaping up and tell his listeners where we are likely to be at various times of the day. He tells me he will catch up with us later in the day, for an in-depth update, he then signs off after wishing us well.

Wally no longer has his Sunday programme on BBC Radio Norfolk.

For the first few years, because of the lack of media coverage we did not have the same number of people lining the route that we have come to expect these days. Every year I have tried in vane to get the local paper to publish a small article about the route that we would be taking and the timetable. Not much of a request, but we never convinced the editor that his readers would benefit from this. I wound myself up so much over this point that I decided to write to the editor in question and give him a piece of my mind. It was bad enough never having our request published, but pushing salt into the open wound was more than I could tolerate.

90

You may recall the earlier mentioned debacle concerning The Country Music Weekend. This very same event commanded a two-page spread every year in the biggest regional paper: the very same paper that we had sent endless requests to regarding our convoy. The theme of my letter to the editor pointed this out in the strongest words that I could find.

I wrote and I remember it well

"Dear Sir,

Every year we have organized and successfully managed to take over seventy five handicapped and underprivileged children on a wonderful day out. We have the support of the police, The Lord Mayor and his office, and thousands of well wishes.

Many people donate large sums of money enabling us to make the children's day ever more special every year.

Every year I write requesting that you publish just a few lines about our timetable; every year you ignore our request.

The very same weekend sees a Country Music event-taking place at Strumpshaw Hall; you somehow find the space for two whole pages complete with pictures.

Obviously money talks."

I also added a few other relevant facts and made it know to the editor that I was fully aware of the fact that the same paper was a major sponsor of the Country Music Weekend. His reply came swiftly back and was along the following lines.

"Dear Mr. Johnson,

How dare you try to influence me or my staff as to what we can and cannot publish in our paper?

I would suggest you arm yourself with all the facts before you make swinging attacks on the local paper or any other form of media.

We have, every year published your request in our evening paper and we consider this to be more than adequate.

Furthermore you do your organization no favours at all by writing such letters."

That told me, did it not?

The point the editor had made about the evening paper was indeed true, but consider this. The Evening News covers less than half of the area we would cover on our journey and it is read by far fewer people than the paper we were trying to get support from.

These days it matters not a jot, we are affluent enough to buy space in the paper.

91

Well before we approach the open road of the A47 we will have passed many hundreds of people lining our route. We pass people waving flags, handkerchiefs and anything else that they can find. We see the first of the hundreds of banners and quickly made signs. Some people are seeing us for the first time, or have just stumbled upon us, and are overwhelmed by the sight that they are witnessing. The first part of our trip takes us past an area in Norwich that has more than its fair share of retirement and nursing homes. As we approach, I can see the staff of these homes wheeling residents and patients out of the sanctuary of their rooms. We just love to see them; even at such an early time in the day they are waving with much vigour and love, bless them.

We as truck drivers on the convoy, all have our own amusing tales to tell about the things that have happened to us on the convoy. My own favourite one still to this day, happened on the first part of our journey. We were but a few hundred yards from Thorpe Green on the outskirts of Norwich. We were making our slow progress past an exclusive apartment block. Young women jumped up to the window to see what on earth was happening. She immediately started to wave enthusiastically to all the truckers and children. It was several seconds before she realized she was completely naked. I can remember her lovely charms burning right into my memory, but not quite as burning as the clip around the ear I received off the present Mrs. Johnson.

Joining the A47, I have a bit of a chance to get my breath back. I make the usual enquiries as to how the convoy is taking shape at the rear; I have excellent feedback from my appointed convoy coordinators and of course, I am in constant touch with our police escort via the police radio loaned to me for the day.

Nearly 45 minutes has passed, since we left the assembly point and still we have only just made the radio masts at Postwick. Our progress is slow but it is safe and already we are starting to look a very impressive sight. The first really amazing sight is about to come into view; my first indication of what we are about to witness comes to me via the police radio; the point man will announce over his radio quite calmly, "Cripes! There are quite a few people on the Blowfield flyover boys!" What an understatement.

The flyover is jam packed with people; they are lined up four and five deep the whole length of the bridge, my heart skips a beat.

"Beat that Strumpshaw", I mutter to myself.

As we make our slow progress towards Acle, it becomes apparent that every year the same faces are in the same places. One group of people are always standing in the same field with a banner that gets bigger and brighter each year. As we go by they are all waving so much you would think they were going to take wings and fly. We approach the roundabout at the far end of the Acle bypass and are clapped and cheered by the crowd of local well wishes.

It is a quiet part of our journey along the Acle Straight or New Road towards Great Yarmouth; save for the usual throng of the people of Halvergate. Every year, without fail, we can expect Betty Tortice with all her friends and family to be waiting for us on the forecourt of what used to be the Stacey Arms. They make the journey down from the village just to see us go by.

The A47 down towards the Breydon is long and very few people will be lining the route at this time of the day. A much different story on the way home. Again, I get in touch with all the convoy coordinators. Satisfied that everything is running properly I remind everybody for the umpteenth time to 'KEEP IT TIGHT'.

This has become the catch phrase of the convoy over the years for the reason explained earlier about car drivers wanting to get in amongst the trucks. Once I am satisfied that everyone is concentrating one hundred percent, I leave it to my number two to take over while I communicate with my point man and ring ahead to our parking coordinators. They will already be at Pleasurewood Hills.

As I make my way over the Breydon Bridge at Great Yarmouth, I will see for the first time the whole length of the convoy stretching back for more than a mile, headlights blazing. They make a very impressive sight. Two hundred yards over the bridge, we look to our left and see a large crowd of people. One person is waving much more than anyone else. Yes, it is my mother, there along with half of the population of Cobholm. The drive from the Vauxhall Holiday Park at Great Yarmouth, all the way through to our final destination of Pleasurewood Hills will be jam packed by now. Every garden, every road junction and any available vantage point would have been filled up well before our arrival.

All of the occupants of the lead truck will be waving and cheering as we go by the hundreds of people. Apart from moments of highest concentration, I too am doing my bit waving and shouting thanks to all the happy people who take the time and trouble to come and see us go by.

As we approach the outskirts of Gorleston the end of the first leg of our journey is in sight. It is but a short hop along the A12 and we are at Pleasurewood Hills. We round the corner into the car park and my first task is to seek out our prepared parking site co-ordinates. Their able team has been led by Gerry King for more years than I care to remember. With so many people milling around it is difficult to spot them immediately but it is not long before I see the fluorescent vests and waving arms, the next bit is down to them, we have arrived.

Lowestoft is the nearest town to Pleasurewood Hills. Unfortunately, the town does not have a Mayor, but they do have a leader of the town council, so we invite him or her along. As is usual with all the dignitaries that we invite as guests to our convoy, they accept with gusto. One of the dignitaries liked us so much when we visited Pleasurewood Hills that, when we converted to a charity, she became a patron. Sandi Kella and her husband Brain are now very valued members of our charity. It gives us a boost and the children feel like VIPs, when public servants like these take an interest in them and our convoy.

We are at The Park until our departure time of about 5.00pm. Up until a few years ago, we used to leave the park a lot earlier to visit the Cobholm Community Centre. It is with mixed emotions and feelings that we no longer go to Cobholm. We decided after twelve convoys that we could no longer go to Cobholm. This was for two reasons, firstly Mother and all her helpers were not getting any younger, catering for over three hundred people was just getting too much for them, although they would not admit to it. Secondly getting our seventy five truck convoy in and out of Cobholm was becoming impossible. If you have ever visited Cobholm you will know the problems that we have had to encounter, the streets are very narrow and the parking was almost none existent. Add to that that there is only one-way in and out and you can see that we have all the makings of organized chaos. After the decision was made to not to visit Cobholm, a delegation from the club made arrangements to tell the residents of Cobholm face to face, rather than just write a letter. We arranged to meet them at the Centre one Saturday evening. We told them why we felt that we could no longer come to Cobholm with our convoy and hoped that they would understand our predicament. We also presented to the residents of Cobholm with a very tasteful plaque, honouring the good work and kindness that they had bestowed upon the children and truckers alike. Sadly, that was the end of another chapter of the convoy; we would never visit Cobholm again.

94

It is much more relaxing for our police escort, the truckers, and I since our decision to stay at Pleasurewood Hills. We have much more time to enjoy all the facilities that the park has to offer.

The management team at Pleasurewood Hills has always treated us as very special visitors and every year they pull out all the stops. One year I was given some extra treatment: more than everyone else was. Although it is not part of Pleasurewood Hills now, Noel Edmunds Crinkly Bottom House Party was a big feature at the park. If you can recall all the mayhem the popular Saturday BBC TV show used to cause, then you will have some idea of what the condensed version was like at Pleasurewood Hills. The show had lots of action, noise, the gunge machine, and of cause Mr. Blobby.

That is where the special treatment that I received came in: no, not Mr. Blobby but the gunge machine. Yes, I was nominated in a covert operation, as the victim to be humiliated in front of hundreds of people. The kids just loved it, and so did my so-called mates.

The park has been considerably modernized over the many years that we have been visiting. In its early years, some of the rides and attractions were a little bit run down. One year some of our larger members had to physically lift a narrow gauge steam engine back on to its track. Some other members were happily messing about in a rowing boat on the lake when the rowing boat started to sink.

5.00pm and our departure time from Pleasurewood Hills comes flying around. Most of our entourage would have been making their way back to the trucks from the indoor concert hall, or Crinkly Bottom as it used to be. I hand out to the management team of the park pieces of memorabilia, and much hugging and shaking of hands concludes our visit. We load up our trucks ready for the off. Our police escort would have been checking that we would not encounter any problems. The leader would have already sent most of the motorcycles out to the main road. When the lead truck appears from the exit to the park the main road is sealed-off so that no traffic is moving when we make our approach.

As we near the main road, it is plain to see that all the media coverage, which we have attracted throughout the day, has now started to have an effect on the amount of people we can expect to see lining our route home. We arrived at the park in the morning, having seen very many people lining the route to the park. We expect to see just as many on our return journey.

What we can never take in is just how many more we see each and every year. The crowds at the first roundabout on leaving Pleasurewood Hills give a good indication of what we can expect on our long and tiring journey back to Norwich. People have come out onto the road; many of them will have been having barbecues. Quite a few have brought out to the bottom of their gardens a bottle or two of wine and as we go by, they toast our passing.

If we had a few quiet parts of our trip in the morning, it gave us the opportunity to rest our arms from constant waving and our mouths from constant smiling. No such privilege on this part of the journey. For the next two hours we will see an estimated seventy thousand people. They will all be waving and cheering with gusto. This free show is rolling and heading for Great Yarmouth and its famous Golden Mile.

On the way to Great Yarmouth, we will see many of the same people who lined our route in the morning. They have brought with them the same love and enthusiasm that they bestowed upon us on our outward trip. Many of the well-wishers would have travelled many miles to see us. It may be the first time for many; they will all be amazed at what they witness. Their reaction is often one of total bewilderment and they will be asking other spectators whatever is this all about. The answer given can only be good, as the following year will see ever more people.

Our return journey through to Great Yarmouth will be exciting to say the least, but the best is yet to come. I can feel a sense of unparalleled excitement starting to envelop the convoy like some kind of buzzing fog; it starts to build just a few yards from where we make our turn on to the start of the Golden Mile. As I make the turn, the point man will be holding the traffic back to give me a clear view of the outstretching road ahead. It always, even after all these years, takes my breath away. I say to myself, "Hold back the tears you chump, you are supposed to be a hard nosed truck driver, not an emotional wreck". I defy anybody not to feel the way I do at this point.

The next thirty minutes will seem to flash by in the click of your fingers. I can see thousands of faces. I am searching for faces that I recognize and I am waving here and waving there. I am looking for someone who said they would be watching us go by at a certain point and I am mesmerized by the numbers of people who have come to wish us and our very special cargo the very best; still I can see only faces, more and more faces. It is like travelling at high speed through a very dense forest; it is impossible to focus on just one of the trees. Then like all good things, it subsides and then it is gone. I am now turning into Lawn Avenue Even though there are still hundreds of people lining our route; it seems to me to be very quiet and quaintly solemn. I am numbed with the crescendo of the last few miles and nothing else will compare with the feelings that I have just experienced.

Every morning before the annual ECT children's convoy, I ask myself the same question "Why oh why do I subject myself to all this worry work and responsibility?"

At about 6.00pm along Great Yarmouth's Golden Mile I have my answer.

If I am damp eyed at this time it is only to be expected, nobody in my truck would notice if I was blabbing like a baby; everybody in the truck with me would have been feeling the same; so would the people in the other seventy five trucks. If you want to experience the same emotional roller coaster come along to Great Yarmouth's Golden Mile on August Bank Holiday Sunday; stand anywhere you can find a space and join in the simple task of expressing love and fondness for people; and they are people who are less fortunate than most. Cynics would ask what all the fuss is about, after all it is only a few trucks and a few handicapped kids; so what? To some degree, the cynics are right; I could not in a million years tell you what we do to bring out the very best in all the people who line our route year in and year out. If there is a magic formula I wish it could be bottled. I would never again have to drive a truck for a living.

The run along the A47 back towards Norwich will see every available lay-by, gateway, and unused field full of waving cheering happy well-wishers.

We, the truckers and our families, are starting to get weary now and by the time we approach Acle most of the children in our care are asleep or pretty well close to it. Our motorcycle escorts have been tireless in their professional execution of their duty. Their attention to detail has seen us through this far without a hitch, or threat of an incident, and the last few miles will be no different.

The sun is starting to sink fast and a red hue is casting long shadows behind us. The multitude of lights the trucks are sporting, are now starting to look ever more impressive. Strung out over a mile the convoy now starts to look like a massive twinkling set of Christmas fairy lights, all be it a noisy one.

Once more, excitement pounds away in my chest as we round the gentle bend of the road along the Blowfield bypass. At first it is difficult

97

to make out what we are seeing due to the suns recent dip behind the concrete and steel structure know as the Blowfield flyover; then we see them. Some of them arrived on the bridge long before we had even left Great Yarmouth. They had set up camp with warm clothes and thermos flasks; they were the lucky ones. Others who arrived a little later would by now be jostling for as good a view as was possible to find. The bridge is over thirty feet wide, two hundred yards long and not a single piece of it is empty.

As I make my approach I let every light I have at my fingertips signal the start of our salute to all these people who make our day what it is. There is no word that I can use to describe how I feel about them, for many hours and days after our convoy people will be heaping praise on the truckers and the club. Quite right too, but if it were not for all the public taking us into their hearts we could not find the energy and enthusiasm to perform this deed every year.

At the end of the Blowfield bypass is one of the last roundabouts that we encounter before we are home. Waving like crazy will be two very special people; there he is our very own Wally Webb, and of course Sheri.

The East Coast Truckers Children's Convoy has been a success story right from the start, even back in the rough-cut days the magic and enthusiasm was there. We have always enjoyed massive public sympathy and support, although I would have liked more general media attention. To be fair, we have always courted a reasonable amount of good will and help from many such organizations. One of these media encounters we will never surpass; the problem was it came with a price. This will be explained in a later section.

Back on our convoy, the tall radio masts at Postwick come into view and I know that the longest part of our day is nearing its end; we are still seeing hundreds of well-wishers lining our final few miles. The sun is sinking fast now and the hundreds of lights on the trucks are a photographers dream. I catch a glimpse now and again and still marvel at the spectacle they all make. I make my approach to the A140 and our final turn into the home straight. I request moderate use of the air horns; check with my number two and the other co-ordinators. My job is very nearly over. As I turn into the entrance of the Livestock Market, (or now days the into the County Hall car park), I am confronted with hundreds of people; most of them will be the families of the truckers and children; the look on their faces is priceless. I neatly park my truck and run over to the entrance to see for the first time the convoy pass in its entirety.

98

Ten hours ago, seventy-five or eighty trucks and three hundred people left Norwich and they are all home safely. For the first time since 5.00 am that morning, I can let myself relax and leave the rest to our army of helpers.

Jackie will have my glass of larger already waiting on the bar of the Norfolk Dumpling, I find a quite corner sit down and thank God, it all went to plan.

NORFOLK POLICE.

Throughout the story of the East Coast Truckers and the convoy, I have on many occasions touched on the subject of the Norfolk Police. It is fair to say that there is a vast amount more to tell.

Sgt Dick Howard appeared on my doorstep all those years ago. His retirement from the force was sad but he was replaced by a man who more than carried on where Dick had left off.

Sgt John Himpleman was a hit with all the children and truckers the first time he took over the convoy from Dick. All the women in the club, according to my wife Mary, thought he was a bit of all right. Apart from his downright good looks, I liked him too.

John made his own stamp on how we were to conduct the convoy and under his direction; it always ran smoothly and looked tidy and professional. He also added his own brand of personalization to the proceedings; in his presence everybody was more relaxed. His coolness and confidence had his team and ours always pulling in the same direction.

At the end of each convoy he would be the first off his bike, and running to where the trucks made their entrance to the Livestock Market, he would stand and applaud all the truck drivers and high five all the kids that would by now be hanging out of the truck windows shouting their heads off.

Every body just loved John.

John was always a big favourite with the club but he has been treated with same respect and kindness as all the other very many policemen who have graced our club since day one.

The special relationship we have with the Norfolk Constabulary is possibly unique; the police forces of other counties would do well to look at how Norfolk could educate them on public relations. I appreciate that we have always conducted ourselves with professionalism and the head sheds at Norfolk Constabulary note this, but the men who help us with our convoy do so not as just a job. They throw themselves into the task allotted to them with no thought about cost or sacrifice. To clarify this point not many people will know that all of our Police motorcycle escort riders perform the job on convoy day without pay. Each and every one of them is on a rest day; they do this because there will always be someone out in the wild, wicked world that will accuse us and the police of wasting tax payer's money.

The job that our escorts carry out on the day of the convoy is absolutely vital. I have to emphasize this point many times but unless you have seen the police in action controlling our convoy, you would be hard pressed to understand exactly what they do. The convoy stretches out the best part of a mile; the police perform three very important roles. Firstly, they keep the convoy rolling constantly. The fewer times you bring the convoy to a halt, the less likely you are to have minor shunts and mishaps. Secondly, they keep other road users well away from us and finally they give the convoy credibility and status. The hardest of these tasks is keeping the convoy rolling; they carry out this task with teamwork and constant referral to me, the convoy leader. With just five bikes, they manage to keep us together and safe. To do this there will be times when they will be coming past the convoy at speeds well over a hundred miles an hour. To see theses lads in action is a pleasure.

Having been a keen motorcyclist myself I am qualified to comment on their riding skills and believe you me they are damn good.

In more recent days, most of the riders were equipped with the far superior Honda motor bikes; in the early days of the convoy they all had to ride the BMW with the horizontally apposed piston configuration; they were heavy, slow and handled like a string vest full of jelly. These true professionals still managed to corner and brake in any weather conditions, faster and smoother than any other road bikers I have seen.

One of my motorcycle mates thought that he could out run the Plod on the Beemer one night when he was scratching along at a fairly illegal speed; the road was wet and on the straight parts of the road my mates bike left the Beemer for dead; what he did not know until that fateful night for him and his licence, was that Plod goes around corners in the wet like they are dry, all down to the training I am told. So be warned!

As with all aspects of our convoy and to some degree the club, there is always a strange or funny tale to tell; our police escorts are no exception. Here are two of the best ones.

100

Earlier I mention the time when the residents of Reedham requested us to run our convoy through their village. As we were making our very slow drive past of the village river front, one of our motorcycle policemen was watching the proceedings from the entrance to a narrow road junction. As I passed by, I could see that our motorcycle cop was doing a bit of posing. He was balancing himself on his bike by hooking one leg over the saddle while the other was planted firmly on the floor. At the same time, he was twisting around looking at the following trucks. As about truck number twelve was passing our poor police officer's foot slipped on the road. He struggled to regain his composure. At the same time, he was battling the effects of a 300-kilo motorbike and gravitational pull. He lost the battle. Eyewitnesses said there was an almighty crunch followed by a fair amount of un-policeman like words and the large bike was lying in the road with a very embarrassed policeman doing his best to upright his machine before too many people had seen his plight. The cruel lot we were, we never let him forget the incident for the rest of that day and on the other later convoys.

The other comical event, although the poor motorist did not see the funny side, happened on the one occasion we took the Children's Convoy to Thrigby Hall Wild Life Park. To get the trucks into the park, we had to go down a very narrow by road. As we were making our way along this tight road, Dick Howard, the point man for the trip went ahead to stop any traffic flying around the blind bend. He stopped in the middle of the road, and when it was all clear, he gave me the nod to proceed. Just as I got to where he was, and where I would turn into the park, a dilapidated car came screeching around the corner very nearly out of control. The car skidded to a halt. The driver could not believe his eyes. Apparently, this poor man had been using this piece of road for umpteen years to go and get his morning paper. The car he had been using for this task did not have tax, insurance, MOT, and all the tyres were bald. When I said the poor motorist could not believe his eyes I meant that he never expected to see five policeman and seventy-five trucks blocking his innocent progress. As Dick said afterwards, "If it were just the tax I would have let him go but the car was a positive health risk". Once again, my request for more media coverage gains credence. If that poor chap had been notified by the regional paper that we were visiting Thrigby Hall, he could have walked after his paper, saved himself a lot of money and avoided an embarrassing court appearance.

I do have one more amusing story regards our police escort. As I mentioned earlier we always run with one police escort rider directly in front of the lead truck. On this particular part of the journey, one year, 'Wes', or Adrian Jarvis as he was christened, was riding point. Where possible we always try to keep to the residential areas. At one point of the convoy on the way home, we could either take the old A12 back to Great Yarmouth, or use the new bypass. We had always used the old A12, Church Lane. I was approaching the roundabout where the two roads meet; I quite rightly was lining up to take the A12 when I noticed Wes turning right; the completely wrong direction. When he looked in his mirrors, he to his horror saw he was all on his own. Red face or what!

I could rattle on for several more paragraphs about our reliance on the Norfolk Constabulary but I think you should by now; have a good idea that they are totally and utterly, indispensable. The East Coast Truckers Children's Convoy can only function with their unswerving help and expertise.

There has been talk that we may have to make some kind of financial contribution to the cost of running the bikes on convoy day; if that is the case then so be it.

I have no doubt that the human resources side of the police will guarantee the same enthusiasm and kindness that they have shown since the day that the long tall ginger figure of Sgt Dick Howard, stood in my door way.

UNITED ROAD TRANSPORT UNION

Over the many years that the East Coast Truckers has been in existence, we have been involved with many organizations and businesses, most of our original contacts with them are still true and strong to this day.

One of these organizations, The United Road Transport Union, has stuck with us through thick and thin since we first struck up an alliance many years ago. (They took over my Charter for Transport, due to the unwarranted muck that was always heading my way because of my political leanings.)

Under the guise and direction of David Higinbottom the union had developed a different approach to the road haulage industry. While the other unions represented several different professions, the URTU supported and represented only employees within road haulage. Every year the URTU will send along to the convoy a top official and their

102

Battle Wagon, and every year we receive a substantial amount from the union coffers by way of sponsorship. In turn, we will always campaign and recruit on their behalf.

We have on numerous occasions approached the URTU either for funds for a charity event or a plug in their bimonthly magazine, 'Wheels'

VARIETY CONCERT.

One event took the East Coast Truckers along a different and new path; a path that was to give us as much satisfaction as the convoy itself.

That event came about by way of a telephone call I received from a truck driver from Bartrums of Diss. The trucker explained that a close relative of his was stricken with the terrible Leukaemia disease. He explained that he and his work mates were looking to raise money to send this little girl to Disney Land in Florida; could the ECT and I help. He also said that he had been in touch with another pal who played in a group, could we get together and try to sort out the best way to raise the money needed?

My first meeting with Bob Maguire was to ascertain exactly what we could achieve and where would be the best venue. We decided to run a variety show; before you could say Jack Sprat my mother was on the phone, "I hear you are thinking about organizing a concert to raise some money. Why not come to Cobholm?" So it was.

We would organize a variety show to be held at Cobholm and we would have to do it within one month. After dozens of frantic phone calls, we finally had more than enough artists to put on a very comprehensive show. Bob and I worked in with mother, and between us, we had worked out a timetable, with time allotted by request, to all the artists. When we had put together the programme, we had thirteen different acts; yes thirteen!

All we had to do now was sell three hundred tickets and find somebody to compare the show and hold it all together. Selling the tickets was no problem. We were sold out well before the event. It was also decided that I should be the one to compare. I had never attempted anything like this before. What the hell, I have no problem talking in public and surely comparing cannot be much different. So on the day of the show, I arrived at Cobholm armed with all my printed matter, timetables and such and a hired tuxedo complete with frilly shirt and bow tie. Dog's dinner was no description.

Bob, mum and Bob's brother were already beavering away; with no fewer than five groups performing on such a small stage, it was going to be an electrical logistics nightmare. Bob had taken full control of all the cables, feeds in and out and junction boxes. Each group had been asked in advance where each particular band member would perform from, so when they finally got on to the stage it would only take a few minutes to connect everything. Easy yes! No!

We timed all the musical acts with non-musical acts between them, thus giving Bob a reasonable amount of time to connect them all up ready for their performance. While the curtains were closed, I would be out front on the dance floor comparing. It was planned that four to five minutes should be sufficient. Did it work like that? Did it hell! After only four acts, I had virtually run out of my previously rehearsed material. I could not blame Bob. We had just gone a bridge too far; nearly every musical act had some kind of problem with their sound system. Bob always managed to solve the problem but each time it was taking longer than the time we had allowed.

Nevertheless all the acts chipped in and some how or other it all came together quite well. One or two of the acts were a little risqué to say the least. I remember one of the acts doing a spoof take off of Andy Pandy. You would not like your children to see the story enacted by the crew we had that night. There was quite a lot of below the belt movement, it was a scream. At the end of the evening we received a standing ovation from the audience. Everybody who had put in so much effort and time said that they had thoroughly enjoyed it and we must do it again. And we would.

The sum of money raised on that one evening topped £1,500. It was put together with all the other money being raised and the total was more than enough to send the little girl and her mother on a once in a life time holiday. Sadly and not long after her trip to Florida, the little girl lost her fight and died.

It was of little comfort I know, but all the people who worked so hard for her on that momentous evening, could tell themselves, that even if they never helped another person for the rest of their lives, they had at least helped one beyond any shadow of doubt.

We considered the concert a real success in so much as we had achieved our objective by raising money for someone less fortunate than our own lucky children. The theme had been set for yet another way for us to lever money out of people's pockets.

We had very little time to put together many concerts but it was agreed by all involved that we would have to repeat the concert in whatever form we could.

For the next three years, we held a concert at Cobholm every six months. We always thought long and hard about the theme for the evening and although we were real novices and amateurs, we put heart and soul into every performance. All the club members would do their bit and I do not think anything else we have ever attempted attracted so much input from the grass root members. There is a well-known saying about everybody has a book in them, I have another theory that everybody wants to be an actor or entertainer; the current popularity of Karaoke would support my feelings.

The input from within the club and our newfound friends from the concert we held to raise money for the little girl with leukaemia, made future concerts an absolute pleasure.

Although hard work, especially after working anything up to seventy hours a week, I never once regretted not even one minute of any concert. We performed a total of six concerts and every one of them was entirely different from the previous one. The children's convoy aside, my life was taken over with constantly dreaming up ever more ways of entertaining up to 250 people. Club members would phone me at 2 o'clock in the morning with an idea that they had to fill a twenty to thirty minute slot in a forth-coming concert; keen or what? Nevertheless, it made my task simpler and even more rewarding. I always think that if people want to do something, they will always do it well.

At one of our concerts, the entire committee of the East Coast Truckers performed a Rugby Player type singsong. If you have never listened to a record of full-blown rugby songs, totally unedited, you must have led a sheltered life. If you have heard them, you will need no description from me as to exactly how rude they are.

Not content with performing the songs to perfection, our lads decided to spice up the visual side to the performance. I will try not to shock too much but one particular song contained a verse describing a very important part of making love to a girl. If I say that they were using liberal amounts of crazy string aerosol from well below the belt I hope you have got the picture, hand gestures completed the obscenities. They had encore after encore; well-done lads.

My mother, as you would have gathered, was never too far away from the proceedings; it would not be an East Coast Truckers Concert without mother being requested to sing. By golly can she belt one out! She did actually audition for the Hughie Green programme "Opportunity Knocks" way back in the seventies but although she had a voice like a nightingale she was too old and not the right shape; our gain, the worlds loss. When mother sings you have little choice but to listen, one of the clubs catch phrases is "don't let mother sing", but all joking aside she has a quite wonderful voice.

As another way to raise money, I hit upon the idea, one concert evening, of volunteering to sing a song if the audience would fill a bottle full of money. Nobody had heard me sing and although I had readily compared all the concerts, singing in public was an area I had never thought about doing. In for a penny in for I pound I thought! I did however cheat just a little bit; the gesture was not on the spur of the moment, as everybody had been lead to believe. I had in fact been rehearsing one particular song over and over again. Having always been a Beatle fan and thinking that I could sing in the same key as Paul McCartney I had been practicing the well-known song "When I'm Sixty four". The bottle was duly filled and all the people who had been waiting for me to fall flat on me face and murder a brilliant classic got a bit of a shock. I am not a terrific singer and I will not be giving up trucking but I can get by, just!

BECOMING A CHARITY.

I touched on the Charity word previously. As this tome has been written over several years quite naturally things will change. The biggest change of all has been the conversion to full charity status. It took quite a long time to achieve this and even after all these years we are still a fledgling charity. At the outset, there were people in the club who were not happy about the conversion; their fears were many but to date unfounded. The charity status has opened many doors and given us immense credibility. Above all, we have good financial standing, which will guarantee that the Convoy will continue for many years to come.

The Herald of Free Enterprise experience gave me a negative view of charities, but Big Rod Green kept repeating to me that we should be a charity. I eventually approached the committee about this. The initial response was not very encouraging to say the least; most of the committee thought that it would be the right way to progress but a few others had serious reservations. One of these was Alison, the treasurer of the day; a formidable woman, you crossed her at your peril, but she was always forthright and honourable. She said that the charity would bring us more problems than we could imagine and that serious divisions were possible. Her fears were proved correct; and we were nearly wiped out.

Rod Green, however, was promising all kinds of inducements saying that doors would open a lot easier with charity status. His argument was a lot stronger than Alison's so off we went.

It took the best part of nine months to get full charity status; still the hard work of Peter Wright, Bill Dewar and I did pay off in the end, and the charity launched officially on Convoy Day.

As Rod had predicted many more doors swung open and it was much easier to get people to give us, not only money, but anything else that we needed. We had funds pouring in and one very kind benefactor sent a cheque for £1,000 after seeing the convoy. She has donated the same amount each year but insisted she must remain anonymous. We were spending the money on a number of good causes; and the convoy, being our main priority, was fully funded and had a budget fit for the purpose.

The charity, under the leadership of Ron, had formed a separate committee, so there was a club committee and a charity committee. The club would have monthly meetings and Rod would attend the club committee meetings to represent the charity committee. The objectives of the charity under Rod's leadership did not always coincide with those of the club, and these often lead to arguments. Eventually it was decided that a vote would take place at the next AGM to ratify the need to be a qualified HGV driver to have an executive committee position. The motion was passed and this meant that Rod could no longer be a member of the committee.

We launched the charity August 2000. As usual, we did not do things by halves; the official launch was announced in the local press and on television and radio. Sadly, we did not get everything as perfect as we would like, and for several months after the Charity was formed some of the worries that some members had started to manifest themselves. We quite wrongly tried to keep the old club alive by running two committees; one for the charity and another one for the club. That was a disaster. When the charity was formed, we quite innocently appointed a separate unelected committee. I was appointed charity secretary, Peter Wright was

Chairman and Tim Thompson was treasurer. Not long after the launch, Peter decided he did not want to be Chairman and resigned. Rod Green asked a woman called Cheryl if she would like the job; she said she did not feel qualified so Rod Green appointed himself as Chairman.

Do not for one moment get me wrong here because Rod Green was one of the most accomplished chairman I have ever had the pleasure to work with; he was articulate, organized and intelligent. Compared to some of our past chairman he was an inspiration. However, his downfall was the very reason he first became involved with our organization. Rod Green was the man who convinced me that the only way forward, not only for our club, but mainly for our convoy was charity status. Of all the people we can look to for the privilege of charity status, Rod had the most influence. It was very sad that he took his eye off the ball and tried to take the charity in a direction that I, and many of the older members, was uncomfortable with. My main concern then, and also right up to the present day, was the protection and prosperity of the convoy. While Rod appreciated the power and attraction of the Convoy, he at the same time wanted to develop a different kind of charity. We had wildly different views on this subject. It was not long before our relationship had started to sour. The turning point was when Rod questioned the purchase of special plaques for the police escort team for the convoy. He made the comment that everyone should be honoured to take part in the convoy and that should be sufficient. What he was trying to do was change the format of the convoy; he would not be allowed to succeed.

It could also be said that a 'them and us' situation was developing within the club/charity. They were pretty bad times. I could see that the only way out of this situation was to go back to just one committee. We had a constitutional ruling in the club stating that you had to be a holder of an HGV licence to be a member of the club. Rod Green did not hold such a licence. If we made the club committee members the controllers of the charity and the trustees then Rod Green could not be elected to serve as its chairman. At the next AGM the floor was given the option to change the constitution while at the same time elect a committee to oversee all aspects of the charity and the club. Rod Green was allowed to state his case and Gerry and Peter pleaded their own case. As it was going to be a close vote Gerry gallantly gave Peter his blessing and stepped out of the bidding. The vote was carried unanimously in Peter Wrights favour. Rod Green was offered the post of President but sadly declined to take up the

108

post. I cannot help feeling that both Rod and the charity lost something that day. Nevertheless, life goes on.

After we had changed the constitution, the opportunity arose to invite non-HGV holders to become full members although we still insisted that each executive committee member would have to be a holder of such a licence. We also encouraged people to become friends of the charity; for £10, they could become more involved and be a part of what was destined to be a fast growing organisation.

It was my idea to have all committee members wear an official shirt and I invented the slogan 'DRIVING YOUR CHARITY HOME'. It was also my idea to extend the membership of the charity and so we launched 'FRIENDS OF THE CHARITY'; if you signed up you would get a gift pack and the chance to win a VIP trip on the convoy. 'Friends' was an immediate success. Again it was my idea to publish a magazine, which would be given to the 'friends' free of charge.

We decided that we should have a logo; the logo would have to be simple in design and easily recognised as being East Coast Tuckers. We asked everybody to submit a design and a vote was to be taken to choose the best. A dead line was set and on the day, we had just one entry! That design became the logo that we have all come to know today.

The convoy was still getting plenty of glory, and every year we ran the convoy we used the term "It cannot get any better", but somehow every year it did just that. Since that first fateful August Bank Holiday Sunday in 1986, the convoy has become part of Norfolk's culture. It is hard to find anybody in Norfolk or Suffolk who has not heard of our charity or our Children's Convoy. There is however much more to do, we still have no major sponsor and everybody we talk to about the convoy finds that hard to believe. On that one Sunday in August, the trucking industry can do no wrong but still no one comes forward with a sponsorship deal. People will ask, "Why do you need a major sponsor when throughout the year funds pour in on the strengths of the public's love of the convoy?" That is of course quite true, but a major sponsor would give us the opportunity to advertise our achievements to a much bigger audience. We could, with the right help double our spectator count; we bill it now as the biggest free show in Norfolk but why stop there? I will never stop trying to get more people to come and wave to our convoy as it makes its way to its two major destinations.

As the charity goes from one success to another, we attract more and more people to give their services free. We now have a group of retired people who enthusiastically promote our achievements.

Mainly due to the success of the convoy and the money it attracts we now take many more children on many more special trips. Only manpower and availability of free time stops us doing even more. We are now attracting a younger element. That is one thing I am very keen to encourage. Our future and that of the convoy is only assured with the help of a younger generation.

EXHIBITION HOSPITALITY TRAILER.

Never wanting to stop moving forward I approached the trustees of the charity with yet another groundbreaking idea. In the course of our fundraising efforts, we accumulated hundreds of pounds worth of stock and equipment. Most of this equipment was stored at a friendly haulage yard and a lot of our property was left with various members; not an ideal state of affairs to say the least. I took my idea first to the trustees and then to the floor.

I had plans, cost estimates, and a comprehensive list of answers to any questions that may be asked. My plan was to build our own exhibition/hospitality trailer. I was talking about a 13-metre step frame trailer. The trustees and the floor gave me unanimous backing and granted me my estimated budget. I was off.

Not one for being afraid of new challenges is all very well but sometimes I wish I was not quite so keen to please everybody and cover new ground. The trailer idea was, even for me, a step just too far. Getting the right trailer was not the hardest part of the project although even that had its problems. What I wanted was a 45-foot GRP step frame; the door configuration would not matter, but it had to have air suspension and good running gear. After trawling through trade magazines, papers, and of course the internet, I finally found one. The trailer fitted the bill exactly; all I had to do was try to get the price down as low as possible. The trailer I found was for sale at Paul Binns International at Huntingdon. I called in on the way back from a trip and looked at the potential purchase. Apart from being aluminium rather that GRP it was just what we wanted. After giving Paul a potted history of the East Coast Truckers Charity, Paul

110

Binns agreed to a substantial reduction in the asking price. I managed to secure the trailer for £2500 plus VAT. Tim Thompson picked up the trailer one Friday afternoon and delivered it to his yard at Attleborough. All I had to do now was find somebody to help me convert it into the planned exhibition trailer. How hard could that be?

I took the plans to the Watling Brothers. They had given much help before so I thought I would start with them. We were not expecting anybody to do the job for free but I did have a fairly tight budget. After careful consideration, they decided the job was too big and in fact they did not think my idea was feasible. Cricky what do I do now?

Panema are a local trailer builder and I thought let's put the plans into them and see what they come up with. They said yes it could be done but it would probably cost £20,000 plus. "Help!   ***!" many expletives came from my mouth. What had I done? Had I wasted £2,500 of hard-earned charity money? Should I resign now, or jump under a truck?

Since moving from Attleborogh in 2004 to live in Mendlesham, my truck was parked at Brian Palmers Transport Yard. Brian is a very clever chap and he is very skilled. In fact, there is not much he cannot turn his hands or his mind to. He also has great affection for our charity. I wondered if he could be the man to build our trailer. I mentioned to him what I had in mind but I did not show him the comprehensive plans that I had drawn up; I was trying not to frighten him off. He asked if I could bring the trailer to his yard so he and his very good friend Dick Hails could size the job up. I took the trailer over to Mendlesham; held my breath and waited for a favourable answer. Brian phoned me one Monday morning and said, "I am sorry Glenn, Dick does not think we could make the structure strong enough to complete your idea". My heart sank, but he carried on, "I will have another chat with him and try and persuade him otherwise". I started to get all religious; God had not heard so much from me in years; yes, I really did need divine intervention. Brian phoned me the next weekend and his words were like honey to a bee. "We will have a go at your trailer Glenn. No I will rephrase that: we will complete the job because if Dick and I start the project it will be done".

Thank you god you have answered my prayers. At last, my dream of the East Coast Truckers Charity having its very own exhibition hospitality trailer was starting to come true.

Brian and Dicks first job was to cut the best part of the whole side out of our recently acquired trailer. This was a very daunting exercise because none of us was qualified as structural engineers. The side was cut out one Saturday afternoon. It was with baited breath that we made the final cut to release a panel eighteen feet wide and eight feet high. It was a great relief when the roofline of the trailer did not move even slightly; a good job well done! The following Saturday saw Brian and Dick start the task of strengthening the side that was now missing a huge chunk of steel. They intended to over engineer at every stage, as the last thing that they wanted was structural problems to develop in years to come. Where the panel was removed, it was intended to construct a drop down door that would also form a stage area or extra hospitality flooring. The part of the trailer where the floor would be jointed to would have to be extremely strong; it would have to take the weight of the door, which had to be extra strong to act as a load bearing stage. When the floor was finished, it would weigh nearly 11 hundredweight, about 500 kilos. Both Brian and Dick were worried that just one door eighteen feet by eight feet would be a bridge too far, so they prudently decided to break the door/floor into two rather than one span. The door/floor was to be lifted into the closed position with the help of two 2000 kilo rated lift winches. These winches were to be mounted in the roof of the trailer; again, special strengthening would be needed, and again this part of the project was to be over engineered.

While Brian and Dick were busy with the task of constructing the doors, I was ripping off the barn doors on the back of the trailer. When the doors were removed, it was my job to replace them with a solid plate steel panel. We did not require a huge rear entry, but we would build a crew door at the very rear on the opposite side to the large drop down doors. After three weeks, the main structural alterations had been finished, and the framework for the doors could be made while the trailer was away having a new coat of paint. We had negotiated with a firm in Norwich called 'Painted That' to paint our trailer for a knock down fee. We did not quite get the price we were hoping for, but the finish on the trailer was exceptionally good. The only problem was that most of the trailer would eventually be covered in sponsor's logos. Never mind we are only truck drivers and sometimes you are going to get things a bit wrong; we learned a valuable lesson with the paint job, never take anything for granted.

With the trailer back from the paint shop, the task of mounting the huge heavy doors was the next on the list. Brian set about making the hinges that would have to support the weight of the doors, and when it was being used as a stage, the weight of several people and equipment. So they just had to be strong. At the same time as Brian and Dick were well

112

into the structural alterations I was busy lining out the inside. Now I was supposed to be building the trailer with help of the whole charity, this was becoming a bit of a joke because very little help ever came. I can mention all of those who did make an appearance and for how long they came and what they done was truly helpful. Tim Thompson was the only member who came for several of the many weeks I was working on the trailer. David Land, Barbara, Colin and Fran also came to help when they could and late in the construction, Roger Weaver helped. Then there was our Wally Webb. He single-handedly made the kitchen; and a very good job he did as well. We secured the help of Shaun and Aaron to wire in all of the electrics and again they did us proud.

Many more hours of work went into our exhibition trailer and I lost count of the times I wish that I had never started the project. Looking back now I see that my idea did hold some water regards helping the charity maintain a larger than life presence. We have always punched well above our weight and the 13-metre bright yellow trailer plastered with our sponsors logos and well wishes demonstrates that in a way that a thousand words cannot.

LINCOLN TRUCKERS CONVOY.

Another organization once tried to emulate our convoy. You will see why we are so thankful and indebted to our Norfolk Police.
Around about 1995 I got into a conversation with a trucker from Lincoln, he was telling me that he had seen a truck convoy taking out children for the day at Great Yarmouth, and asked if I know anything about it. He could not have got a better man! We arranged to meet his team of organizers at Frankie's Café on the A17 near Long Sutton one Saturday Afternoon.

On the appointed day, I arrived with some volunteers from our team to meet with the people from Lincoln. They had expressed a wish to run a convoy similar to ours in Lincolnshire; they needed our help and expertise. We spent the whole afternoon giving them as much advice as was possible and they were frantically taking notes as fast as they could write.

The one thing we did put much emphasis on was the fact that they must have the support of the police. Without this vital piece of help, they would never succeed in operating a safe well run convoy. How true our words were!

113

The following year we were notified by our friends from Lincoln that they were going to run a convoy from a little place called Kirton to the seaside holiday resort of Skegness. The convoy was scheduled to run on the Easter Sunday.

A team of supporters from Norfolk made their way out to Lincoln to give help and encouragement wherever we could. We never interfered or criticized. We only gave help.

After the first day, we could see it was doomed to fail. Why? Because the Lincolnshire Police had no interest in the convoy's aims.

The group had assembled the trucks at the Village Hall and a well-known local celebrity had been invited along to officiate; actually, he was the infamous Eric Pollard from Emmerdale, the television soap.

Once we had seen the convoy load up and get ready for the off, we chased off to find a good vantage point to watch and cheer the convoy on its merry way. We run our convoy on direction of the police controllers and over the years, we have settled on a maximum convoy speed of 30mph. There is a very good reason for this. We have, over the years, run our convoy at varying speeds but we have settled on 30mph because of the length of the convoy. Basically, when you are stretched out over such a large distance and you have seventy five other trucks with you, it becomes impossible to keep them altogether. The front dozen or so trucks may be travelling at 40mph but the trucks further back may only be doing 10mph.

It is a time-tested practice and 30mph has been deemed as the ideal speed for our convoy.

We, the East Coast Truckers observers, set our selves up in a lay-by about half way between the Village of Kirton and the final destination of Skegness. Cameras at the ready we heard the convoy making its way towards us. I poised myself ready to get some good shots. Too late, I think I may have taken three photographs. Within seconds the convoy had passed. Fast or what?

The reason for this fast fly-by was that the organizers had been told by the police, that if they caused any traffic hold ups at all, they would be booked for obstruction. They were also told that no police help would be given at any time. Funny thing was the police did send along two traffic patrol cars and I saw at least three panda cars along the specified route!

Just to digress here and get something else off my chest. Lincolnshire has a rather large concentration of speed cameras on its roads; very many of them are set to catch speeding trucks in areas I would not call one little bit hazardous. A phrase from the film Convoy comes to mind here, "My name is patrolman Jones sir and I hate Truckers".

The organizers at Lincoln struggled on against adversity and eventually gracefully gave up after three years. As a consolation, we always invite one of their trucks along to our own convoy. You can see why we value our own police and hold them with such high regard.

EVERY ONE LOVES THE CONVOY!

Sadly, that has not strictly speaking always been the whole truth. I remember with horror a very serious incident some years ago.

For one year and only one year, we took the convoy with its usual precious cargo to Fritton Lake. Fritton Lake is situated about halfway between Gorleston- On- Sea and Beccles. The convoy was about two miles from the entrance to the park, when over the CB came a message. I could not believe what I was hearing! The conversation from a rather upset trucker went like this.

"Some loon just came out of his house and lobbed a ruddy great big brick at my truck". The CB was naturally alive with disbelieving enquiries as to the full story.

One of our golden rules is, no matter what happens, the convoy only stops on direction of the police controllers. We true to form carried on the last few miles to where we were parking for our visit. The truck that had been struck came into view with its rather flustered and angry trucker at the wheel. Just above the radiator grill a very large dent was evident, along with a spider's web like crack in the windscreen, just a few inches higher and it would have caused serious injuries to the occupants of the truck.

Sgt Dick Howard inspected the damage, interviewed the trucker and between the three of us we decided to go back to the area where the brick was thrown. The trucker identified the house from where he saw the brick thrower appear. Dick knocked on the door; it was a good five minutes before a, very sheepish looking, women answered the constant knock and persistence of our now angry policeman. She explained that her husband was not in and had not been there for the whole day. Our trucker was quite certain that the brick thrower was a man.

We left without really achieving anything, so Dick agreed that he would go back to the address unannounced at a later date.

Two weeks later Dick rang me to tell me that he had interviewed the brick thrower. His bizarre statement left little doubt that the brick thrower was severely deranged. Apparently, he was an avid canary breeder and our large noisy convoy was upsetting his birds. Not much of an excuse to unleash a deadly missile at innocent people, I admit it could have been much worse.

Dick asked if we wanted to press charges, I contacted the owner of the truck, he in turn said that the damage was superficial and the matter was closed as far as he was concerned. I too, was happy to see the end to the whole sorry affair.

So you see not everybody loves the East Coast Truckers Children's Convoy

Another person who would rather have not seen our convoy was the driver of a solo artic unit making his way home one very wet Sunday morning. As explained these tractor units are designed to operate with a heavily laden trailer, take the trailer away and you lose more than seventy percent of your braking response, as this poor chap discovered making his way back to his depot.

It was on one of the very few occasions when we had a wet start while running our convoy. I thank God for that. As we were making our way along Church Lane at Gorleston, the solo tractor was making its way towards us on the single piece of soaking wet carriageway. Having never actually spoken to the poor chap driving the truck I can only assume what happened. As he came down the hill, the sight of all these trucks with lights and horns blaring must have totally mesmerized him.

He over braked approaching the roundabout, veered violently to the left, demolished a garden wall, and stopped with his front bumper wedged up against the door of what once was a very tidy house. Now that, in itself, must have been quite an horrendous experience. Couple that with the embarrassment he must have been feeling as seventy five fellow truckers trundle by at what must have seen to him to be a painfully slow process, would you have wanted to be in his shoes? I know what my answer would be.

MORE TELEVISION.

David Hannington was the television producer who was responsible for the earlier mentioned documentary on young Heidi. You will recall she was the seriously handicapped girl who sued her own mother for a record insurance settlement. David wrote to me expressing a desire to research the feasible likelihood of us, the East Coast Truckers helping with a documentary about the plight of the English truck driver. He could not have picked a better bloke. I have always had more than my fair share to say about the way we are depicted, treated and reimbursed for our toils.

I spent several hours on the phone to David, giving him a very good insight into the workings of the haulage industry.

David had convinced his superiors that a documentary about truckers would be of public interest and so it was. After our conversation, David considered it worth taking to the next level.

He also wanted to see the industry for himself warts and all. He arranged to spend a few days riding with me in my truck, making notes and observations. He explained to me his desire for me to give it to him as it was and not to dress the job up in any way what so ever.

He was to regret his wish to see and live the job as a trucker would. We were on our way back from Birmingham after having delivered a load of cargo. We were getting a little peckish so I suggested stopping for a bite to eat. Not being allowed to stop at Little Chefs or such like, because if you are in a truck you are sub human, I told David the only place we would be likely to get a cuppa and a snack would be one of the lay-by tea bars that have sprung up all over the place since the demise of the traditional transport cafes. So, as I made my way along the link road between the M6 and the M1 near Rugby, we came upon a scruffy converted caravan. Don't ask what it had been converted into, because if the designer was trying to make a café he had missed the target!

We opened the door to be greeted by an unshaven slob of a man. His once white coat was only held together by ancient egg, beans and grease stains. As we closed the door behind us, he stubbed out a very wet dog end and greeted us with, "What's it to be governor?" David said with his very Oxford accent, "What fare has you on your menu my man?" That threw the slob, "I have sausages, bacon or burgers and that's it mate".

David inquired as to what I was having and promptly ordered the same. A cup of tea and a sausage sandwich looked about the safest bet. Our slob chucked a tea bag into each of two cups he had fished out from somewhere near the discarded dog end. He poured hot water into the cups and then squeezed the tea bags with his nicotine stained fingers. David's face was a picture. The sausage sandwich was delivered with much the same aplomb as the tea, a piece of kitchen roll was wrapped around a deep fried gristle filled sorry excuse for a sausage sandwich; only the bread

117

could be called anything like palatable. It was admittedly hand cut and fresh, even if it was twice as thick one end as it was the other. I managed to eat most of mine; David almost consumed half of his. We left the shack silently.

Once on the move David said, "Are all the places you eat in like that?" I replied, "Not quite as bad, but it is typical. We do have to have to eat in some really bad joints". The sting in the tail to David's first sample of British trucking was this. He was due to visit Lords Cricket Ground the day after his delightful introduction to trucker's cuisine. He had been given two tickets for a test match. The next time I spoke to David, I naturally enquired as to how his day at Lords had been.
"I never made it", he said. "Oh! Why?" I asked. "I spent the best part of the day on and off the flaming toilet", he explained. He continued, "My backside was trying to re-enact Vesuvius and my mouth was in competition with my rear end." I had to stifle a laugh.
"How are you?" he said. "I'm fine; no trouble at all", was my reply.
He muttered something about cast iron guts, made his excuses and put the phone down rather hurriedly. Poor David; but it did make my case even stronger as to what a crap life we truckers put up with.

A few weeks after David had submitted his initial findings to the hierarchy of the BBC, David and his crew started filming.
His crew was a cameraman, sound engineer, a research assistant and an absolutely stunning blonde called Jane West. The first day's filming was to take place on one of my many trips to Wetherby in West Yorkshire. It was intended that the crew, along with David and Jane, would meet me one Monday morning at about twenty miles from Wetherby. I left my home that morning at 3 am. They were all holed up in a very cosy hotel on the Sunday afternoon.
Mind you, it was worth it. Jane looked deliciously stunning even at 7.00.am

For the next four weeks, David and his film crew would meet me in various locations. We would go over and over the same thing, take after take after sodden take. I am no stranger to the workings of Television and Radio, but this time it was starting to wear me down.
Finally, David said that he had enough in the can. They were going into editing and eventually production and he would let me know when the documentary was to be televised.

The programme was televised on a Thursday evening on BBC 2 directly after Eastenders had finished on BBC1. Prime slot or what eh!

118

2005 Fundraising at Cobholm Community Centre. From the left: Keith Postle. unknown,Michael Jeal. David Yallop, Nigel Folkard,Betty Tortice, Sue Robinson, Doreen Johnson, Glenn Johnson.

119

Peter Wright presenting Betty Tortice with a trophy for 15 + years involvement with the East Coast Truckers

Top: Andy Tait, Past President and Rob Billman. Bottom: View from the cab of spectators on the A47 in 2010.(Teresa Wilce)

121

Top: Trucks arriving at County Hall and being booked in for the 2010 convoy.
Bottom: County Hall Car park with trucks lined up ready for the off.
(Teresa Wilce)

East Coast Truckers fund raising at the Forum in Norwich.
(Teresa Wilce)

2011 Children's Convoy. Top: trucks lined up in County Hall Car park in early morning. Bottom: Breakfast stall at 7:30 am at County Hall. (Teresa Wilce)

Harly Marrison with his carer / grandmother Chris King. (Teresa Wilce)

Norfolk Gala Day at Royal Norfolk Showground in 2011

The programme had more than just highlighted problems within our crap industry. It had turned over some very dark and dirty stones. I had been allowed to air some fairly strong views and a very activist kind of politics was starting to creep into my way of thinking. I did not know at the time how dangerous this political angle was about to become.

The programme was very astute in it is no nonsense approach to all the grievances I and many of my contemporaries had made. The producers had been very careful to seek views from all sides of the industry. The programme came over as fair, honest and very thought provoking.

Directly after the programme was aired, I was to be taking part in a live BBC radio programme, which was to conduct a kind of inquest into the findings of the subject matter. The next day my phone never stopped ringing. "Fantastic. Well done. It is about time someone told the world about our plight. Now let us tell them even more of what we have to put up with. Go for it Glenn. Do not stop now", were just a few of the comments and feedback I was receiving. I was the industries champion over night.

PAYING THE PRICE.

Much earlier in this story, I explained that the East Coast Truckers had very nearly been killed off twice. I also said that the Television programme came at a price.

Well here comes my own personal horror story. It started with all the previously mentioned glory but ended with me in a hospital bed with metal plates and screws holding my face together.

The trouble first flared up after one of our Sunday morning club meetings where I was chairing a discussion about the television programme transmitted the previous week. Part of the discussion centred on comments that I and other contributors to the programme had made about percentage payments to truck drivers.

Under EEC tachograph rules and regulations it is an illegal practice to pay truck drivers any form of performance related wage.

Percentage wages were therefore deemed as illegal payments to truckers. This point had been clarified several times before but some people were still missing the point I was trying to make. By way of an explanation I mentioned by name, a few local hauliers that had favoured this method of payment.

127

I had made the statement at a private gathering, but I would regret that act for a very long time!

Within but a few hours of the regrettable statement, it had been leaked completely out of context by someone to one of the local hauliers I had mentioned. That haulier in turn had repeated the comments that I had made, again out of context, to two of the other hauliers and so the poison word had spread.

In my opinion, nobody had really listened to what I had said. Instead, they had interpreted my statements to their own end and advantage. One theory is that if a boss does not want his staff to negotiate for a higher wage he will find a way of frightening staff into thinking that his or her job is at risk. Many of the local hauliers had tapped into that method and now they could use my attack on them as fuel for the fire. Many of them had told truck drivers that if they had to pay them in the legal and traditional way i.e. hours and overtime, they would all lose their jobs.

Where did all this leave me? Truck drivers champion one minute, villain of the piece the next. My life for the next several years was affected, not so much by what I said but by what people reported me as saying.

What could I do? You can only stand your ground and argue your case if you have someone to confront. All of my adversaries would spread the poison and run.

I had to find a way of minimizing the damage to not only myself but to the convoy and the club alike. Firstly, the Charter for Transport that I had been working on with two other like-minded colleagues was handed over to The United Road Transport Union and all political comments regards the East Coast Truckers was to be handled by anybody other than me. Still people were using me as the local whipping post.

The firm I contracted for was told by the local hauliers who had taken great offence to my comments that I was not to be trusted because it was my intention to bring down all people who depended on transport. I was accused of preaching anarchy and treason. I only managed to keep the work that I had been doing well for several years, by the intervention of

Brian Weatherly, who was the much-esteemed editor in chief of a trade journal for road transport; The Commercial Motor. He threatened the firm whom I hauled for, that if my work was in any way jeopardized because of the truthful comments that I had made, he would make damned sure that bad press was the least they could expect. The firm concerned backed off, but not before I was warned that if I continued along this very disruptive political path, I would find myself looking for alternative work. Getting nasty is it not?

There was much, much worse to come.

My prized and treasured truck had been vandalized; everywhere I went some trucker would make derisory comments and if ever I walked into a gathering of truck drivers, it was as if the plague had descended on them.

There was a campaign being conducted to slur me and slag me off at every available opportunity. Not only that, the club was being dragged into the quagmire along with me. The lies that I was constantly hearing from some of the true friends that I had managed to keep, were frightening and upsetting. I had never said any of the things that I was being accused of. All I could do now was weather the storm and hope that the knockers and mockers would get fed up and move on to something or someone else.

One comment that I was reported to have made was quite damming. I was reported to have said, "That drivers running bent or over their permitted hours were the scum of the earth". What I had said was, "Haulage contractors who force or encourage their drivers to run bent should be stopped and severely dealt with by the authorities governing road haulage". Quite different I hope you will agree.   If you were one of the hauliers my comments were aimed at, it would be in your own interest to make your drivers think that I had said something derisory about my own kind.

Still it got worse.   Previously   I   mentioned   the   good relationship that the club had with local business. I mentioned with great pride Duffields, the massive Volvo dealer, and the good terms we had with the whole organization. Someone decided that he would put a spoke in the wheel here. Just because he had a few Volvos he thought it would be a good idea to sour our relationship by suggesting that he might just take his custom somewhere else, good man.

Another haulier muddied the waters with the local Renault dealer; and so the nightmare continued.

About the dirtiest trick was pulled by a quite despicable person. He, I was reliably informed is still seething even right up to the present day about the comments I made about hauliers all those years ago. To harbour a grudge for so long borders on the insane, obviously the truth hurt this haulier more than anyone will ever know. Our despicable friend had told his drivers that they were forbidden to have anything to do with the East Coast Truckers or their convoy. He was obviously a tyrant as well. I though we were all free men, not so if you were unfortunate enough to work for this character. He threatened all his staff with instant dismissal, if any of them were to go against his wishes. His hatred of the club and me was now starting to get totally out of hand.

One of his drivers approached me about two months before the Children's Convoy. He was pushing his luck by even talking to me. He said, "Glenn is it OK to put a truck in the convoy this year?"
My reply was, "I thought you had been forbidden from taking part ever again!" "Do not worry about him I am going to take part whether he likes it or not", he said. I explained that I, nor the club, wanted any more trouble than we already had but I would consider his request.

At the next committee meeting, I mentioned the request from this particular driver. A fair debate was conducted and it was decided that because he was still a member of the club he had every right to take part in our convoy. So be it. The driver would obviously not be using a truck from 'Dick Dastardlys' fleet, so I found the man a truck from a good friend of mine called Paul Alderton (better known as RockHead). I thought that would be the end of it. On the day of the convoy, the driver came up to me and said that he thought that he would be looking for a job the day after the convoy. "Why?" I inquired. Our local tyrant had told his driver that he would be following the convoy and if he saw our man taking part he could get the East Coast Truckers to find him another job. One of our major sponsors is the United Road Transport Union. They always attend our convoy, so I directed our man in their direction. There are supposed to be laws protecting us from petty Hitlers. I was sure that they would solve the problem.

Sure enough, the driver turned up for work on the Tuesday morning and was promptly sacked on the spot. I could not believe that anyone could be quite so heartless, uncaring and despicable.
Unfortunately for 'Dick Dastardly' one of the handicapped children's parents got to hear of the dastardly deed and informed the local paper. The

local paper told the tabloids; the tabloids told the Television companies and they in turn told the radio stations.

'Dick Dastardly' was infamous overnight; his front garden looked like the front of 10 Downing Street during a crisis meeting of the cabinet.

Reporters were everywhere. Dick Dastardly was a wriggling now! Somebody called the local radio station and pleaded Dastardly's case by saying that he had nothing against handicapped or underprivileged children. I gather he was a vilified object of hate for many months to come. Tough!

A few months afterwards, the foray over the sad deed had died away. Our trucker, who had unceremoniously been sacked, had found another job and some of the flack seemed to be getting thinner. Dick Dastardly was still trying to patch up his ruined reputation and chucking the odd threat here and the odd threat there.

Alas, history has shown he may just have got in the last kick.

You will remember my remarks about ending up in a hospital bed with a face full of screws and plates; well it was not an accident! I was being presented with the keys of a brand new truck that Mary and I had just taken delivery of, at the premises of a local dealer.

There were about eight people present at the small ceremony; when into the compound came a man known to me and most of the rest of our party. He uttered a few derogatory words. I approached him with the desire for an explanation. Knowing this man's reputation as a bullyboy and a thug, I was certainly not going to confront this man with anything other than words. My stance was in no way threatening and if you have seen me, you could not describe me as 'Bull in a China Shop' material. The next thing I knew I was sliding across the tarmac on my side; the camera I was holding hit the floor in a dozen pieces. I tried to stand up but my legs had taken a holiday. When I came to my senses, I could hear the wail of a distant ambulance. People were fussing about all over the place and now I could feel something in my mouth that should not have been there.

I had been hit so hard that the whole side of my face had been stoved in, hence the plates and screws. The Maxilo Facial Unit of the Norfolk and Norwich Hospital put right the damage, and apart from setting airport metal detectors off there was no lasting damage.

My assailant received a laughable punishment. Why did he do it? Only he can tell you the answer to that difficult question. If I could give you a clue, it would be this. The man who threw the punch was in my view primed, cajoled and convinced by persons who shall remain

131

nameless, that it would be in every body's interest to smack that evil Glenn Johnson. A bit like the man Who Shot Liberty Valance, he thought he would be the hero of the day. Some people just do not want peace. I hope and pray that this sad chapter is now long dead and buried.

From here on in to the end of our long but unfinished story, it is mostly good and upbeat. Some of the afore-mentioned hauliers accepted the olive branch we so desperately sent out as often as possible; the others shot the dove and snapped the twig. We do not need them in fact they can go to hell in a handcart. I, and the East Coast Truckers, learned a very valuable lesson; leave politics to those who are stupid and big enough to handle the fall out. We as a club, and I as a person, will never venture along that road ever again. My views and principles will, however, always be the same. I think it was Winston Churchill who said, "Principles are a very expensive but necessary part of any civilization". I would certainly agree with the word expensive.

Of the hauliers that we did find our peace with: the relationship is now as good as ever. In fact, one of the hauliers has become a major contributor and benefactor. Bill Watling and Sons had as big an axe as anybody to grind with the East Coast Truckers and me but we have come of age and together we are much stronger. The family firm of Bill Watling and Sons was started more years ago than can be counted on an abacus. It was run by two of the sons, Timothy and Christopher. Joy and Bill Watling have retired from the day-to-day running of the haulage business. (Since writing began on this story Bill Watling has sadly died) Joy Watling even through the dark days of the previous chapter, always secretly contributed money and help towards our convoy

The high profile trucks the company ran were admired by all who saw them, in every corner of the British Isles and more recently Europe. It was an honour and a privileged to have such an eye-catching fleet on our convoy. Many thanks to the whole family!

LAST CHAPTER

The convoy grew in popularity and esteem year on year, and the public awareness was just more than I could ever imagine. Little did we know that the convoy's popularity with everybody would also become a thorn in its side. We had always prided ourselves on safety; not only for our precious cargo, the trucks and all of our entourage, but also for all of the thousands of people who came to see the convoy rumble past.

This attention to detail regarding safety resulted in us asking for a total road closure along Great Yarmouth's Marine Parade. The Highways Agency and Norfolk County Council were consulted and convoy 23 saw us with our first ever road closure. That was not to be the end of our quest for safety; the local authorities, including our good friends the Police, were not happy about existing arrangements. This prompted a meeting between all of the interested parties. The aim was to prevent a problem or accident well before it could happen. The outcome, although satisfactory to everybody, was only to be short lived.

By the time of the convoy 26 the end was looking ever more like a very sad possibility.

In 2010 we would be running our 25th convoy. Wherever did all those years go?

I had imagined many times what the 25th convoy would be like; but like all dreams, they cost money.

Just like when the convoy started, a little piece of divine intervention was required. It came by way of a bequest. A very kind and generous lady had witnessed the convoy many times as it passed by the vicinity where she lived. She had gotten so much joy from seeing the convoy that she had written into her will that we should receive a large amount of money when she died. When Mary Reeve sadly died, she left £86,000 to our charity.

My hopes were raised! I would be able to run and organize the special kind of convoy I had envisaged. However, true to form it would not be that simple. The convoy had grown so much that the organizing team now ran to many people.

The money left to us by our very kind benefactor became as much a problem, or hindrance, as it did a welcome injection of funds. Because many people had a hand in the running of the charity, a clear and united idea of how the money should be spent became impossible.

I approached the floor at a monthly meeting and put forward proposals of how I saw the 25th convoy and how much I thought it would cost. I informed the membership of some of my ideas; I rightly pointed out to the membership that Mary Reeve had donated the money because of the convoy and that the convoy should be the event to gain from the windfall. The proposals were debated at length and a vote was taken. The membership unanimously agreed that a sum of £25,000 would be made available to fund one massive tribute to our fantastic milestone.

Sounds great you may think! Not so! Within only days, tiny-minded people were protesting that the money should not be wasted on our 25th convoy. Wasted! Wasted! If I had not witnessed all of the other sad occurrences in my life regards the convoy I would have never believed such a spiteful, ignorant and pitiful statement could be made by anybody.

Without the convoy, the charity would have never existed and the East Coast Truckers Club would have gone the same way as the other 5000 or so other CB clubs that sprang up in the early 1980s. So how could somebody make such a statement?

Easy, you just join an organization that managed quite well without your help or hindrance for many years and then you cause mayhem, controversy, and sow seeds of doubt, hoping that your destructive ploy will have the desired effect.

The problem for me was that the destructive interfering moronic minority that had festered itself upon my beloved convoy had to some degree won.

Rod Filmer; yep Rod Filmer; know him? You may if you are a truck driver; if you are not a truck driver or a member of his family or a friend you would have never heard of him. But I got a call from one of our regular convoy drivers telling me that a Rod Filmer would like to come on our convoy. So I got in touch with this Rod Filmer and asked him if he would like to join us on August Bank Holiday Sunday. He did not have a clue what I was on about, so I contacted the chap who had told me about Rod Filmer. "You deaf old ****; his name is Rob Billman. O.K."

"Hi Rob" I said on the phone

"How would you like to come on my Children's Convoy?"

That was the start of a long and very good relationship that will never be sullied, or spoiled; even by the most vicious of actions or perverse accusations by others. We are frank with each other; we talk and debate every thing imaginable; and above all, we have the same mindset. His first ever Convoy was a more life changing experience that he or his lovely family could ever imagine. I may have made his life better or I could have made it worse but change it I did.

The day after his first convoy, he called me on the phone and delivered one of the nicest, comprehensive and sincere thanks you that I have ever had.

After a few weeks of talking regularly on the phone I gathered there was a great deal more to this guy than first meets the eye.

For some time I had been trying to convince myself that it was time to call it a day as Convoy Director, and hand the reigns over to a younger person. Have I found a likely candidate? I had nothing to loose, so I dropped the question in one of our conversations.

I think he was quietly stunned. Maybe he was flattered, or maybe he was thinking why me. However, after a few days of mulling it over with his family he said yes, he would love to work along side me for the next two years.

"Hello everyone this is Rob Billman your new Assistant Convoy Director", I announced to a very well attended meeting.

Controversy has always been my middle name so why start trying to be different now. The members of my anti-fan club as usual protested after the meeting in their little huddles. Their only concern was who is this Rob Billman? Hold on chaps and chapetts you will find out in the next two years, and I do not think you are going to be happy.

Rob did not only start to learn and take on board all of the many aspects of the convoy; he threw himself into the role with enthusiasm and a keenness that I had gradually lost over the years. He was also making himself wider know within the charity and he had definite aims to join the executive committee. Personally, I thought he was taking on too much and I told him so, on many occasions, to reign back a little. But, who was I to tell him what to do. He was, and still is, his own man. Many people, in my little anti-fan club, had assumed that Rob would merely be Glenn Johnson's puppet. They could have never been further from the truth.

History, and the future, will demonstrate my point with more clarity than I can write here.

We did have, however, a very bitter few weeks, which tested our relationship to its absolute limits.

Rob had been a good contributor to a truck driver's forum where anybody with an interest regards trucks and road haulage could vent their spleen. I too became a regular contributor and posted many thought provoking topics; and yes, true to my character, controversial. One such post pointed out to the forum that the road haulage industry still had its fair share of cowboy or bad operators. I went a little further than some people would have liked, I did not use any names as the forum forbade this kind of action, but I cleverly worded the post making it perfectly obvious who I was referring to. There was uproar from the three main guilty parties; *let them that are guilty shout their innocence the loudest thinks me!*

Rob, however, became the target of the uproar because of his links to me, and the three louses in question brought all of the venom and hate right to his door. Why they never came after me, I will never know, although I do have my suspicions. One of the people was shouting so loud he might as well have owned up to the crimes there and then. Having had several bad experiences with this man before, I knew that his guilt would not let him rest until he had sought retribution on someone or anyone. He and his cohorts protested to the forum's administrators and had the offending post removed. Rob was being bashed verbally from several directions and he finally snapped. He, in my view, wrongly approached the man who was shouting the loudest and tried to apologize on behalf of the charity, but still no abuse had come my way. Rob then turned his attention towards me, and I duly explained to him that it was my battle and not his. I was quite strong in my choice of words resulting in both of us falling out pretty damn bad.

It was looking like I was back to looking for a suitable successor. Andy Tait who had taken over from me as the President of the charity began to mediate for all he was worth. He understood the spat that I had had for many years with the main protagonist. He also agreed with my opinions and views, and he knew the full sorry story. Andy brokered a meeting between Rob and myself, and, along with a few other committee members, we sat down to try to sort out the dilemma that we had found ourselves in.

Although we did not cover much ground at that meeting, both Rob and I learned a valuable lesson. A few days later both Rob and myself spoke on the phone; we agreed that the only winner in the whole fiasco resulting in our partnership failing would be the protagonist. We were not about to let that happen. We are now more resolute in our understanding of each other and the mutual respect we have, sees us through any problems that may come our way.

So I have my successor! It is time to sit back and enjoy my last two years at the sharp end! Yes, I know, I spoke far too soon.

Back to the tiny-minded brigade: earlier I had made everybody aware that I wanted the 25th Convoy to be spectacular, special, and really put us on the local map in a way that we could never have done before. Why could we not achieve this before? The answer is because we never had any money. Now we did have some money; money, which was rightly

136

donated to, and for, our convoy. The tiny-minded shortsighted critics that I have always had to dodge around were in top gear, setting cluster bombs of dissention everywhere.

In complete contrast to the little group of people with nothing much to occupy their minds, the Charity, and again in particular the convoy, encouraged and enthused people to come forward with good ideas and very good intentions. Two very good examples of this kind of enthusiastic person were Simon and Danny who started up a very good Truck Rally based in the southern area of our charity. Simon Waspe and Danielle Harvey had been thinking about organizing and running a Truck Rally and a Spit and Polish competition for many years. In 2007, they finally put it all together. They held the first two rallies at the Crowfield Rose Public House and so it became known as the Crowfield Rally.

Simon and Danny worked their respective socks off to make it a success: they encountered many problems but, through it all, succeeded and made it work. The first Rally started just fine, but half way through the prize giving the heavens opened, and opened, and opened. It became so bad that half of the trucks attending had to be winched and towed off from the quagmire that was once a solid green field. The second rally faired a little better, weather wise, but was still not perfect. The weather, however, was not the main problem.

The big problem was the same one that I had regarding the managing of the convoy; namely too many interfering, egotistical and ignorant people trying to get their opinion above all others, including the people who had the original idea. Simon and Danny promised themselves that they would not put up with the pain in the backside that I had to endure. Yes they told all and sundry that the Rally would in future be run by them and them alone.

While I had set Rob to work on his first task on the 24th convoy, I put my mind and all of my imaginative energy into finding ways to achieve my desire and dreams for convoy 25. At the same time the plotters were hard at work trying to achieve the very opposite. My original program for convoy 25 was completely ruined by the time the 25th convoy had come upon us.

Rob had done a terrific job on the 24th convoy and completely down hearted rather than exhausted, I handed over the complete running of convoy 25 to him.

It was a baptism of fire; he had first to get around all of the new directives and laws covering recent road closure applications. He also was running

137

the first ever 100 truck convoy and he was trying to fight my corner with the tiny-minded brigade.

Yes that is right I did say 100 trucks.

It was while Rob and I were in a meeting with our escort group at Pleasurwood Hills that we dropped the bombshell to our Police escort group leaders.

Andy Spall and Adrian Jarvis had worked very closely with me for many years, and because of their professionalism, the convoy always ran smooth, trouble free and with the kind of aplomb that only police motorcycle riders can deliver.

We dropped into our conversation with Andy and Adrian that we would like to, just for the 25th convoy, run 100 trucks plus the usual support vehicles. Bracing ourselves for a strong rebuff, we took a deep breath. Andy calmly said, "No problem", and that was that. Phew!

How ironic it is to find that all of the people outside our charity do their utmost to help us, and always surprise me with the lengths they will go to solve problems and give me the encouragement to succeed.

On the other hand, we have our charity! There are more cases of dissention regards the charity, and some of its members, than I have time, or inclination, to bother with but I will tell of the one case that will sum up all of the others.

Part of my plans for the 25th convoy was a commemorative jacket; each trucker who would drive a truck on the 25th convoy would receive one of these uniquely designed jackets. The jacket would be of excellent quality, tasteful and instantly recognizable as a 25th convoy celebration jacket. They would cost approximately £50. The fall out and shouting of objections about these jackets was unbelievable. There were cries of "What a waste of money!" from the dissenters, "How dare that Johnson throw our money away on Driver's Jackets?" "Who the hell does he think he is?" and so on!

I have always stood by the same defensive argument regarding the criticism that came my way about this 'bone of contention', and it is this:

Keep in mind that the protesters had never put even one gallon of diesel into a convoy truck in all of their sorry lives! I will explain to anybody who cares to listen, that most people, and mainly those that tried to destroy my 25th convoy, that to prepare and run a truck on our convoy to the standard required, costs on average each trucker no less than £100. That is not including any time off work he may have taken to get the truck ready. It is not including the money he may spend on the child in his care. Then there is the man hours preparing a working truck for our big day.

Where did these people come from and why do they end up giving me a headache? If I sound bitter, it is because I am bitter. I will never forgive the protagonists; I will never forget how they very nearly ruined 25 years of hard work.

It is for that reason and that reason alone that my involvement with the charity is now minimal.

The systematic destruction of my host of plans and dreams were made even harder to bear because of the loss of a dear friend and President of the Charity.

I have already mentioned Andy Tait; remember the Mud Wrestling and him being a go between just recently. Andy was with me from the very first day of the convoy. He volunteered to take over the running of the convoy for one year; he helped with all of the concerts we put on at Cobholm and if you go all the way back to the first lines of this story he was the man talking on the CB about the very first meeting of the ECT. He was also the man who filled the vacancy that I had left when I stepped down as President of the charity.

To loose such a very good, trusted, and esteemed friend was a terrible wrench to put it mildly.

It was not long after Andy had helped put Rob and I back together that he called me on the phone one afternoon. I knew that he was visiting the hospital for tests but I always looked at him as being indestructible, so I was not unduly concerned.

After Andy's call, my assumptions were wrong, totally wrong! Andy said in a soft and slightly trembling voice, "I've bloody well got it". He continued, "Just been to the hospital and the doctors have told me I have cancer". I was numbed. The man I had come to think of as always being there was telling me that soon he would be gone.

I will always remember Andy as a blonde, blue eyed, mischievous, larger than life character. His help with our concerts was immeasurable. His act was clever; he had a great voice and he could sing a Neil Sedaka classic called 'OH CAROL'; half way through this rendition he would slip into his NORMAN WISDOM character; hilarious is an understatement. His involvement with all aspects of the club and then with the charity, and of course the convoy, was always understated, because he was quiet and always in the background. Not everyone appreciated how much he actually achieved. He also befriended a man of

139

the cloth called Geoff Brendling; he persuaded Geoff to come along to a meeting, and low and behold, Geoff loved us so much that he became our Padre.

Andy deteriorated very quickly; Rob and myself feared he would not be well enough to take part in the 24th convoy. Rob arranged for a good friend of Andy, Gordon Covell, to take Andy on the convoy if he was to be well enough. Rob made a golf buggy available for him at Pleasurewood Hills. Thankfully, Andy made it to the 24th convoy. It was a few weeks later that Andy very sadly died. By golly, I will miss him!

Andy's family and friends organized a benefit memorial ball and all of the proceeds went towards buying a fitting memorial for Andy. We approached the management of Pleasurewood Hills to see if it would be possible to have a memorial sited at their Park. They happily agreed and a large granite picnic table was installed for all people visiting the attraction to use.

Andy was never aware of the problems that continued to dog me and the other members of my organizing team, he and his family had much more to worry and concern them.

Rob was doing a very good job on all fronts of the convoy; he was living up to all of my expectations. He learned very quickly how to get the best from all around him; he learned that not everybody will be on the same page as him and he learned that an articulate and informed argument always wins the day. His rapport with everybody that he has to deal with is exemplary. He will always put his newfound skills down to my coaxing and teaching but you have to have the metal to start with. He is not short of that, and by golly, does he need it!

So convoy 25, and my last at the sharp end, was looming up with enormous speed. My own life had been a high-speed rollercoaster of events and I was looking forward to an end to the responsibility of running the convoy. I was also looking forward to living my life in a much less confrontational environment.

I have always been resilient to criticism and dissention about how I had run the convoy. I have always parried the attacks with the time-aged claim that on the day, I always deliver and no one has ever been able to say different. That is what gets up my attackers noses more than anything else does.

The 25th convoy, in spite of all the trouble that I had had in the early planning stages, came good. Many of the thorns in my side had failed to complete their dirty deeds, and better still, they had moved on.

The weather could have been much better but that was the only flaw in the day. We had our one hundred trucks, and immaculately turned out they were too. The children will never forget the spectacle; the truckers, their families, and I will never forget the spectacle; but most of all the thousands of people who braved the weather will never forget it.

As I complained earlier: much of my original programme had been pulled apart by the tiny-minded brigade. What remained was still good, and the final drive into County Hall with me as lead truck was just magic. I had booked the Norwich Pipe Band to lead us back into County Hall, and as I approached Martineau Lane, my heart was racing harder than it had done all day. The pinnacle, to something that was arranged for just one year, was for me ending after 25 long years. I had been terrified of this moment in my life because the convoy had been a very large part of my life for a quarter of a century. In that time I have seen my sons grow up, get married, have children, I have been to hell and back fighting a succession a people who I can only describe as serial protagonists. Now it was all coming to an end. Happy? Or Sad? I really do not know, but a relief of some kind it certainly was. As I parked my truck for the last time at the head of the convoy and wandered into County Hall, I was full of good happy memories. In spite of everything, I have had a wonderful experience; I can go to my grave knowing that I had made a little bit of difference to many peoples lives. I had given deserving children an experience that few other charity organizations have the ability to do. I had given ordinary people a purpose of worth and importance.

Where will the charity go now? Will it continue to survive when many others of the same size flounder and die? If my beloved convoy has to stop because of the relentless march of the dreaded Health and Safety brigade, can the charity find an alternative event?

Many questions! But there is hope. The charity has a man who has the same ability as I had all those years ago; that is the ability to see a long way into the future, a man who will not be perturbed by the small minded blinkered brigade, a man who given the freedom can possibly find a way. That man is my successor and good friend Rob Billman. Help him and flourish; or lose him and die!

I had been at the birth and construction of a humble club, I had given that club a purpose to survive, and I had been at the forefront in the conception of the registered charity it had become. Now I want to see it flourish and become my legacy.

Mum was also stepping down. She had decided that she too was starting to feel her age. My brother Carl who had always supported all my efforts and also helped on every convoy we had run was also calling it a day. The Johnson reign is coming to the end.

I believe many of the old convoy regulars will also call it a day. Who can blame them it is not getting any easier.

All that polishing and all that waving does take its toll.

Will I miss it all!!

'Keep It Tight'

EPILOGUE.
An inevitably concise update on the significant events that have occurred at East Coast Truckers since the Club became a Charity.
By
MIKE READ

It was in due in no small measure to the work of some-time President Rod Green that an application to become a charity was made. One way or another, the Convoy had soldiered on and managed to take place every year. A Christmas party was added to the timetable of fun provided for the children. After becoming a charity the next outing that became a semi-permanent feature was an annual trip to Africa Alive. But, not much else was possible because, basically, the kitty was empty.

Achieving charitable status in July 2000 was no immediate financial panacea, but it did plant the first step in establishing the credibility and awareness that East Coast Truckers was an organisation that had graduated from being a drivers' club where resources were pooled to pay fines incurred as a result of using CB radios to providing for the needs of disabled and disadvantaged children. Apparently, after each convoy there had been a frantic fundraising effort just to pay the bills that had been incurred. That had to change.

The first landmark in establishing our future recognition occurred on 10th April 2002 when several ECTC members attended the fifth Civic Award Ceremony at the Norwich City Hall. Jane Dewar had successfully nominated the East Coast Truckers Charity for one of two group awards which were presented by the Lord Mayor of Norwich, Kenneth Ratcliffe. This award was for unsung heroes who selflessly dedicated their lives to helping those in need within the community. The Lord Mayor was quoted as saying "These people go about their work with no thought of recognition or reward. Their dedication is inspiring and it lifts the spirits to meet them".

Peter Wright, the then-chairman added, "The work we do has its own rewards, but it is great to be recognised in this".

In terms of promotional tools, the next great leap forward was the 19th Convoy in 2004. A first class video was produced with Radio Norfolk's Wally Webb doing the commentary and interviews. This piece of cinematic history has been used on countless occasions since and has been seen by thousands of people at Truckers' presentations. For many people seeing this film was the first time that they had any idea of the work that our charity does. Its success was really proven when, the year afterwards Norfolk County Council agreed to host the start and finish of the Convoy from County Hall. Not only was this a relief for us all because of the imminent closure of the Hall Road cattle market site but was also a tremendous boost to our prestige as an up and coming organisation.

Becoming a charity does not have all the financial benefits that you might expect. Contrary to general belief, we pay VAT like everyone else. But it does convey a certain status and it is always helpful when negotiating a discount with suppliers to mention that "we are a charity".

Publicity is the oxygen of success and, quite clearly, the Convoy is and will, hopefully, remain our flagship event. The light suddenly dawns with people who know nothing about us as soon as the convoy is mentioned. And, it is also to Glenn's credit that he came up with the idea of the Exhibition Trailer. It was a brave financial decision to decide to embark on this project. But, today, it is another part of East Coast Truckers that is instantly recognised wherever it goes.

Add in countless presentations by our team to members of the public from all walks of life, which started off as a one-man talk and a showing of the 19th Convoy video to a South Norfolk wine circle and you have a winning publicity formula.

Where does this get us? Well, financially, it gets us quite a long way. To date something approaching ninety thousand pounds have come in over the years from people who have seen us at work and have remembered us in their Wills. One very large legacy spawned the ECTC Holiday Homes. 2011 saw the launching of 2 large static caravans at California Cliffs, near Gt. Yarmouth. In a full season about 50 families will enjoy a week's seaside holiday totally free of charge.

Grants have also come in from some unexpected sources and, very often, local clubs and businesses have raised money for ECT as their sponsored charity of the year. It would be invidious to name those concerned as, inevitably some would be left out. Everyone who has taken the trouble to raise money for us from a nationally-known supermarket which is a household name, through to a fun pub for gays, a Norwich night club, rural social clubs and literally dozens of W.I.s and other focus groups of one sort or another, know who they are and what they did. Our thanks go out to you all.

144

So, what does East Coast Truckers do with the money these days? What it doesn't do is pay wages. We are all volunteers and, although those whose responsibilities that do create a great deal of out-of-pocket expenses get a modest mileage allowance, for example, administration costs overall including postage, auditing fees etc. amount to only 8% of our revenue.

The rest is spent on "Delivering Loads of Fun to Special Children". One of the early new events came courtesy of Attleborough Players who run a pantomime every January at the Connaught Hall. There was, they admit themselves, hesitancy when they found that they were to play before an audience of children, many of whom have a great deal of difficulty in understanding what is happening. After the first performance the Players decided that lack of mental capability was not bar to the total enjoyment that the children experienced. These days, the children get their own dedicated matinee performance and the Players swear that this is the best show of the season.

Other outings also take place. We have tried railway trips in North Norfolk, Banham Zoo, Teddy Bears Picnic, Gt. Yarmouth Hippodrome Circus, and Banger Racing for some of the children. We are always looking for new things to try but any suggestion must always be thoroughly risk-assessed and carefully considered with regard to the children's safety. And, most of all, are they going to enjoy it?

We do have to try to spread the money around as effectively as possible. We aim for maximum benefit to a maximum number of children. But, occasionally, we do step in to help small groups of individuals or even a single child. This very often takes the form of a genuine hard luck case like the Jenny Lind children's unit at the Norfolk and Norwich hospital that suffered the theft of about a dozen Play Stations. Reading about this callous crime in the local press we were able to buy replacements and get them into use before Christmas. Quite a number of children have the need for a highly specialised wheelchair that the State simply won't fund. The reasons often revolve around the length of time the child will get the benefit from it. We've got round that problem with an example that the State would do well to copy. When we can we will buy, or with money raised by the family concerned or another charity's contribution, help to buy an expensive wheelchair. But, here's the difference. We take them back in when the child outgrows the chair or has no further need of it for any reason. It goes back to the manufacturer for a

145

complete overhaul and re-emerges almost indistinguishable from new for another child to use.

So the £5000 price tag on some of these units looks a little less expensive when, over the course of time, with a few service tweaks on the way, that chair may serve many children. In this way we have accumulated a small "equipment library" from which we can often draw a bit of kit that might otherwise be denied to a deserving child.

We are an "as well as" rather than an "instead of" organisation as far as goods that could be state-funded are concerned. We do check-out requests, especially for individuals, to make sure that we aren't being asked to pay for something that could be state-funded. If necessary we will point people in the right direction to get the help they need elsewhere. But sometimes we help where, frankly, the State is an Ass. Take the child with a life threatening brain deformity, which could be cured with a treatment and special helmet that costs around £2000. Although the State will fund having a child's ears pinned back, the brain problem is classed as "cosmetic". We don't think that a life or death brain condition is cosmetic so we dived in and paid for that treatment within a day or two of reading about the family's predicament.

From major help like this to providing a professionally made wig for a little girl with severe facial and other deformities caused in an horrendous house fire. This wasn't a life or death issue. It was just to help her sense of dignity as she became a young woman. Call it delivering loads of fun, if you like. These are the kinds of things we do; whenever we can.

One thing that has gone unmentioned and can also be attributed to the early ideas of Rod Green is the "Friends of East Coast Truckers". Originally, a member had to have or have held an HGV or PSV licence. This rule was altered but there were still a large number of people who took an interest in our charity but weren't inclined or, indeed, in a position to be a full-blown member. These days the "Friends" number in the hundreds and the print run of the ECTC Tymes now approaches 800 as this is the number needed to make sure everyone gets a copy.

This brings us to people. We have a trailer; we have gazebos, barbecues, wheelchairs, cameras, DVDs etc. etc. But our greatest asset is our people. The strength of East Coast Truckers is seen in the faces of people who show up at our monthly meetings and in the dozens who turn out for events, fundraisers, promotions, children's days out, doing the accounts, managing the merchandise, writing the magazine, taking the

146

photos, dealing with the Inland Revenue and the countless other activities that go on relentlessly by an army of volunteers who make themselves responsible for running this wonderful organisation. The result does credit to them all and, in the 21st century this Charity is a monument to dedication and selfless hard work all for the love of children less fortunate than us. Few can have foreseen in 2002 when the Lord Mayor of Norwich Kenneth Ratcliffe uttered those words of praise for the Truckers that the Charity would grow the way it has. The more we continue to grow the more fun we will continue to deliver to our special children.

BETTY TORTICE – FRIEND OF THE TRUCKERS.

I became involved with East Coast Truckers soon after the convoys began, after I met Doreen Johnson at a party in Winterton. She gave me her telephone number and her son Glenn's number.

My family and friends then got together and organised fetes and discos and raised funds whenever we could. Over the years, I have made cakes, sausage rolls and other things for numerous events, which include the convoys and children's Christmas parties.

Over my years helping with the charity events I have received several awards. When the convoy had its twentieth year, I, along with several other voluntary helpers, was given an award for fifteen plus years service. I also received a 'Special Friends' award in 2007 at the Children's Christmas Party held at the Marina Centre in Great Yarmouth. Another 'Special Friends' award followed in 2008.

ECTC TYMES

BY
MIKE READ. CO-EDITOR

Issue No. 4   Charity Reg. No. 1082023   Spring / Summer 2005

We're Driving your Charity Home

It was in August 2003 when the "ECTC Tymes" was born. In those days the plan was to produce, at most, a quarterly publication whose format would be the traditional "coffee table magazine" size with a good deal of colour content. This was fine but had two fundamental flaws. Layout and printing had to be done professionally and, as such, it was expensive to produce. Additionally, there already was an established need for something like a newsletter. With the growing number of "Friends" who, unlike members, did not attend monthly meetings, it was apparent that a far more frequent publication was needed to keep them up to date with what the Truckers were up to.

Our charity was growing in both size and prestige so we quickly discounted the idea of a monochrome newssheet in favour of the now-familiar A5 part-colour, nicely bound, mini-magazine.

It is published about nine or 10 times a year and for the 25th Convoy, a special extra commemorative edition was produced.

ECTC collects donations and money from fundraising, merchandise etc. in order to finance our various activities "Delivering Loads of Fun to Special Children". Moreover, it is our proud boast that apart from about 8% of our annual income, which covers insurance and other administration costs, everything that we collect is spent on the children. Therefore, it was decided that ECTC Tymes needed to be self-

148

financing. Therefore, we have been very dependent on the sponsorship that we receive from our various advertisers.

In these difficult financial times, sponsorship finance is not easily come by so a small annual subsidy is provided from the East Coast Truckers' Club. The Club derives no money from the funds collected by the Charity for the children and derives its independent income from membership subscriptions, raffles and other fundraising events at social gatherings for the members. In return, all club members and, of course, the "Friends" receive their magazine absolutely free of charge.

Issue Six   Registered Charity No. 1082023   2006

CHARITY   MAGAZINE

Obviously, we could not sustain this situation if professional printing costs were involved. Therefore, co-editor Ivan Hardy set up all the equipment required to print, cut, fold and staple our regular print run, which is now nudging 800 copies. This is a time-consuming exercise and, apart from Ivan's work, having mastered the "Quark" publishing programme, in producing the layout, there is also a dedicated team who meet about once a month to put the thing together. This is labour intensive. However, without this invaluable labour, ECTC Tymes could no longer operate as a free magazine.

Apart from keeping everyone aware of what's coming up in "Dates for your Diary" (As an aside, I can remember the first edition going out with the typo "Dates for your Dairy", but our proof reading wasn't so thorough in those days), the magazine provides a platform for publicising all the varied activities that occur during the course of the year. In addition, whilst we try not to make an account of an outing a list of "Thank You's", it is important that members who do give up a great deal of their free time get the recognition they richly deserve.

I would like to report that ECTC Tymes goes from strength to strength but the future is far less certain than that. It is becoming increasingly difficult to keep the project self-financing and, ultimately, it will be for the Trustees to decide what the future will be.

But, for now, we can look back on 8 years of producing something that falls short of being as glamorous as a Sunday newspaper supplement, but, in our humble opinion, is far too good to be dismissed a just a "newsletter".

MY FIRST CONVOY

BY
TERESA WILCE

Having only moved to the Norfolk area back in March 2010, I signed on with an agency and my first job was working for Bartrums. Within a couple of weeks I had met Gerry and Prinny, who, both on the same day, said that if I wanted to meet people in the area, I should join the East Coast Truckers, advice I duly took and signed on in May. By this time, the preparations for the 25th convoy were well under way. Having worked for many years in administration, prior to my "mid-life crisis" of becoming a driver, I was immediately impressed at how organised the club was and the way that members worked together as a team for the common end. It was like being part of a huge family. I quickly found myself being caught up in the excitement of the event.

As I was new to the club I could only sit back and watch as the preparations were done with the precision of a well-oiled machine, although I did have a lot of fun helping at peripheral events such as the Costessey Fete and the Forum, where I could wander around trying to part the public from their money.

The weekend of the Convoy arrived with; it seemed to me, a mixture of excitement and apprehension. Had everything been covered? Was everyone sure they knew their places and what actions they would need to take? Had the truck been polished to perfection? Now what can possibly go wrong...? Mark out the truck parking spaces, go for a Chinese; we are counting down the hours.

6am on the 29th August 2010 – 25TH CONVOY DAY – it is freezing cold, overcast and buzzing with activity at County Hall. Final polishing of trucks, reception areas being set up for both children and drivers, burger van in place with the kettle on for breakfast – the arrival of hungry children, parents and truck drivers is imminent. As the first trucks arrive, Vic and her team quickly move them to their parking place, designed to ensure that all trucks leave in numeric sequence as smoothly as possible, the parking area fills steadily whilst children begin arriving excited at the thought of going on a big lorry. Despite the cold day, everyone is in good spirits and the public begin turning out to watch the amazing spectacle of 100 trucks, with air horns and lights blazing, smiling children at the windows leaving for Pleasurewood Hills.

10am and the start of the convoy is signalled by white doves being released, the trucks begin to roll, uncoiling from their parking spaces like an enormous snake, I hop aboard the coach, secretly wishing I was driving one of the trucks, a lump in my throat at the sight.

All the way to Pleasurewood Hills, the sight is incredible, so many people flaunting the cold weather to cheer the convoy on, smiling and waving flags. At least it is not raining! I spoke to soon......

The rain waited just long enough for the first children and drivers to go aloft on the chair lift and then threw buckets at them, but even this could not dampen the spirits and the smiles continued all afternoon, well once wet we might as well get wetter, so let us go on the water slide.... Or the boats..... Or anything else that

Takes our fancy..... And here is the picnic, cakes and drinks and all sorts of goodies, just what hungry bellies need before climbing aboard the trucks once more to make the journey back.

All along Yarmouth sea front the crowds are waiting, the convoy is a special event for everyone, adults and children alike, and no matter how much the wind blows off the sea, the smiles bring out the sunshine for all of us.

Arriving back at County Hall, I help with reuniting the children with their families, along with all sorts of goodies to remind them of their day. Although it has been a long day, the smiles are still firmly in place and everyone agrees it has been a wonderful day.

Finally it is time to go home, I go to bed and fall asleep with one leg still on the floor, the day of my first convoy is over and I can't wait 'til next year to do it all again.

TAIL END CHARLIE

BY
DAVID LAND

The saying used to be "Last but not Least". In convoy terms, however, it is as in the title. Yes, just plain 'Tail End Charlie'; but, believe it or not, it means more than you think. I was asked about six years ago if I minded being at the back. I said "No".

Really, in simple terms, you are eyes for the convoy director who is in the front truck. I can contact the director via telephone or CB. So, on the day at 10 o'clock away we go. I sit and watch as all the trucks leave just waiting for my turn.

When I eventually leave, I tell the front that the convoy has now completely left County Hall. Slowly we wind our way down towards Lowestoft through Thorpe and on to the A47 keeping an eye out for any pullouts which happen from time to time. Then it is down to me to inform the front what is happening and, if possible, bring them back in. There is only one point in the journey at which I can see the whole convoy. This is on the Acle Straight. The leaders are going over the new Breydon Bridge and I am half way between Stracey Arms and Vauxhall Caravan Park and what a sight this is.   When we arrive at Pleasurewood Hills, we get parked up ready for departure at 5.15 pm. Once again, leaving in the evening, I notify the front that for the second time the convoy is totally mobile heading for Yarmouth seafront. With lights and horns blowing, we slowly wind our way through with me reporting now and again to say all is O.K. at the back. The journey back is much the same as earlier in the day. With just as many people watching we arrive back at County Hall and another convoy comes to an end with, best of all, happy children, parents, and truckers.

SUSAN ALABASTER CHILD LIAISON OFFICER

Saturday night 2nd October 2010, saw members of East Coast Truckers Children's' Charity, family and friends join together at Cobholm Community Centre to celebrate the 25th Children's Convoy and looking back what an eventful last few years it had been. There had been the trips with the children to the circus, pantomime, Dinosaur Park, Santa Pod, Stock Car Racing. We had been on Teddy Bear Hunts and taken part in the Lord Mayors Parade, attended fetes at various places, had Saturdays at The Forum. Then there is the Children's Christmas Party, when Father Christmas arrives in a splendid truck, fitting for man of such great importance.

Of course there has been the social side for members and their families as well. Quiz nights, bingo, party nights, boat trips, the Annual Christmas Dinner Dance and not to forget the pre-Convoy Chinese meal.

But it is the trips with the children that stay with me. I have been involved with E.C.T.C.C. for the last five years and have met some wonderful children, all special in their own way. Spending the day with them is fantastic and seeing the enjoyment they get from their day out is the best reward you can ever have. The Pantomime is always good fun as not only are the children fully involved but the adults throw themselves into it as well. The calling outs of "he's behind you" always seem to come from 'older' members of the audience!

The Convoy itself is amazing, and nothing prepared me for my first one. Yes, I knew the children were taken to Pleasurewood Hills for the day, went on the rides and had a tea. Yes, I knew there was the procession along Great Yarmouth seafront, but it was the reaction from the public that took my breath away. The streets, roadsides, bridges were lined with people cheering, waving and holding up banners and that was just going to Pleasurewood Hills. The return journey via the seafront was so emotional. It was just a sea of well wishers, you cannot really explain it and do it justice properly, it is something that you need to experience to fully appreciate the impact that the Children's Convoy has on people, from the very young to the elderly. The cheers from the families when we arrived back at County Hall said it all. The 'Special Guest' you take out becomes part of your family for the day and when the day comes to a close the greatest thanks you can have is from that child when they give you a big hug, nothing compares to that.

There is, of course, a lot of hard work that goes on behind the scenes to make the Convoy and the outings happen. Coaches have to be booked, letters to parents sent out, venues booked, plus various other sundry items organized and in the case of the Children's Christmas Party there are presents to be bought and wrapped. As for the Convoy, there is months of planning and organization that go into it, but when the day comes, wherever we are going or what we are doing, when you get to the end, the smiles and happiness of all the children say it all.

As the last few years have passed I have got to know quite a lot of the children and their families, more so as I am now the Child Liaison Officer, but looking back to that night in October, when we celebrated the anniversary of the 25th Children's Convoy it was, in a way, an end of an era. The directorship of the Convoy was handed over and the catering for the children on Convoy Day was also handed over. Glenn Johnson stepped down as the Convoy Director and his mum, Doreen Johnson, stepped down from the catering. What a brilliant son and mother team. Thank you both so much for all that you have done.

BECOME A FRIEND

If you, or someone you know, would like to get involved and become a Friend of the East Coast Truckers' Charity then here is what to do. Send a minimum of £10.00 (less than 20 pence per week), and you will become a Friend for a year. In return, the East Coast Truckers will send you a Friends Welcome Pack

The charity has no employees; the expenses are kept to a minimum; so nearly all your donation goes to benefit the children of East Anglia, including a Christmas Party, a trip to the Circus, Pantomime, an Easter Outing, a trip to Santa Pod, a trip to "Africa Alive" and to run the Children's Convoy, or to obtain merchandise for sale to generate more funds.

So join now, send your donation to:

EAST COAST TRUCKERS' CHARITY
FREEPOST P.O.BOX 56,
ATTLEBOROUGH, NORFOLK, NR17 2WT.

THANK YOU
To get involved and become a Member apply for an application form from our Member's Secretary at the free post address above.

Other books by Sheila Hutchinson:

THE HALVERGATE FLEET:
PAST & PRESENT

BERNEY ARMS
REMEMBERED

BURGH CASTLE
REMEMBERED

REEDHAM
REMEMBERED

REEDHAM
MEMORIES

THE LOWER BURE
FROM GREAT YARMOUTH TO UPTON

THE RIVER YARE:
BREYDON & BEYOND

FREETHORPE
PAST & PRESENT

Sheila Hutchinson

Berney Arms: Past & Present, 2000. (Out of Print)
The Halvergate Fleet Past & Present, 2001, ISBN0954168305. (Out of Print)
The Island (The Haddiscoe Island). Past & Present, 2002, ISBN 0954168313 (Out of Print)
Berney Arms Remembered, 2003, ISBN0954168321. (Out of Print)
Burgh Castle Remembered, 2005, ISBN0954168833X. (Out of Print)
Reedham Remembered, 2006, ISBN0954168348
Reedham Memories, 2007, ISBN9780954168353. (Out of Print)
The Lower Bure from Great Yarmouth to Upton. 2008, ISBN9780954168360.
The River Yare: Breydon & Beyond. 2010. ISBN 9780954168377
Freethorpe Past & Present 2011, ISBN9780954168384